Spark Cookbook

Over 60 recipes on Spark, covering Spark Core, Spark SQL, Spark Streaming, MLlib, and GraphX libraries

special gift for Antonio
Remember us for Spark needs

Rishi Yadav

[PACKT] PUBLISHING
open source
community experience distilled

BIRMINGHAM - MUMBAI

Spark Cookbook

First published: July 2015

Production reference: 2220715

Published by Packt Publishing Ltd.
Livery Place
35 Livery Street
Birmingham B3 2PB, UK.

ISBN 978-1-78398-706-1

www.packtpub.com

Cover image by: InfoObjects design team

Credits

Author
Rishi Yadav

Reviewers
Thomas W. Dinsmore
Cheng Lian
Amir Sedighi

Commissioning Editor
Kunal Parikh

Acquisition Editors
Shaon Basu
Neha Nagwekar

Content Development Editor
Ritika Singh

Technical Editor
Ankita Thakur

Copy Editors
Ameesha Smith-Green
Swati Priya

Project Coordinator
Milton Dsouza

Proofreader
Safis Editing

Indexer
Mariammal Chettiyar

Graphics
Sheetal Aute

Production Coordinator
Nilesh R. Mohite

Cover Work
Nilesh R. Mohite

About the Author

Rishi Yadav has 17 years of experience in designing and developing enterprise applications. He is an open source software expert and advises American companies on big data trends. Rishi was honored as one of Silicon Valley's 40 under 40 in 2014. He finished his bachelor's degree at the prestigious Indian Institute of Technology (IIT) Delhi in 1998.

About 10 years ago, Rishi started InfoObjects, a company that helps data-driven businesses gain new insights into data.

InfoObjects combines the power of open source and big data to solve business challenges for its clients and has a special focus on Apache Spark. The company has been on the Inc. 5000 list of the fastest growing companies for 4 years in a row. InfoObjects has also been awarded with the #1 best place to work in the Bay Area in 2014 and 2015.

Rishi is an open source contributor and active blogger.

My special thanks go to my better half, Anjali, for putting up with the long, arduous hours that were added to my already swamped schedule; our 8 year old son, Vedant, who tracked my progress on a daily basis; InfoObjects' CTO and my business partner, Sudhir Jangir, for leading the big data effort in the company; Helma Zargarian, Yogesh Chandani, Animesh Chauhan, and Katie Nelson for running operations skillfully so that I could focus on this book; and our internal review team, especially Arivoli Tirouvingadame, Lalit Shravage, and Sanjay Shroff, for helping with the review. I could not have written without your support. I would also like to thank Marcel Izumi for putting together amazing graphics.

About the Reviewers

Thomas W. Dinsmore is an independent consultant, offering product advisory services to analytic software vendors. To this role, he brings 30 years of experience, delivering analytics solutions to enterprises around the world. He uniquely combines hands-on analytics experience with the ability to lead analytic projects and interpret results.

Thomas' previous services include roles with SAS, IBM, The Boston Consulting Group, PricewaterhouseCoopers, and Oliver Wyman.

Thomas coauthored *Modern Analytics Methodologies* and *Advanced Analytics Methodologies*, published in 2014 by Pearson FT Press, and is under contract for a forthcoming book on business analytics from Apress. He publishes The Big Analytics Blog at `www.thomaswdinsmore.com`.

I would like to thank the entire editorial and production team at Packt Publishing, who work tirelessly to bring out quality books to the public.

Cheng Lian is a Chinese software engineer and Apache Spark committer from Databricks. His major technical interests include big data analytics, distributed systems, and functional programming languages.

Cheng is also the translator of the Chinese edition of *Erlang and OTP in Action* and *Concurrent Programming in Erlang (Part I)*.

I would like to thank Yi Tian from AsiaInfo for helping me review some parts of *Chapter 6, Getting Started with Machine Learning Using MLlib*.

Amir Sedighi is an experienced software engineer, a keen learner, and a creative problem solver. His experience spans a wide range of software development areas, including cross-platform development, big data processing and data streaming, information retrieval, and machine learning. He is a big data lecturer and expert, working in Iran. He holds a bachelor's and master's degree in software engineering. Amir is currently the CEO of Rayanesh Dadegan Ekbatan, the company he cofounded in 2013 after several years of designing and implementing distributed big data and data streaming solutions for private sector companies.

I would like to thank the entire team at Packt Publishing, who work hard to bring awesomeness to the books and the readers' professional life.

Table of Contents

Preface

The success of Hadoop as a big data platform raised user expectations, both in terms of solving different analytics challenges as well as reducing latency. Various tools evolved over time, but when Apache Spark came, it provided one single runtime to address all these challenges. It eliminated the need to combine multiple tools with their own challenges and learning curves. By using memory for persistent storage besides compute, Apache Spark eliminates the need to store intermedia data in disk and increases processing speed up to 100 times. It also provides a single runtime, which addresses various analytics needs such as machine-learning and real-time streaming using various libraries.

This book covers the installation and configuration of Apache Spark and building solutions using Spark Core, Spark SQL, Spark Streaming, MLlib, and GraphX libraries.

> For more information on this book's recipes, please visit `infoobjects.com/spark-cookbook`.

What this book covers

Chapter 1, Getting Started with Apache Spark, explains how to install Spark on various environments and cluster managers.

Chapter 2, Developing Applications with Spark, talks about developing Spark applications on different IDEs and using different build tools.

Chapter 3, External Data Sources, covers how to read and write to various data sources.

Chapter 4, Spark SQL, takes you through the Spark SQL module that helps you to access the Spark functionality using the SQL interface.

Chapter 5, Spark Streaming, explores the Spark Streaming library to analyze data from real-time data sources, such as Kafka.

Chapter 6, Getting Started with Machine Learning Using MLlib, covers an introduction to machine learning and basic artifacts such as vectors and matrices.

Chapter 7, Supervised Learning with MLlib – Regression, walks through supervised learning when the outcome variable is continuous.

Chapter 8, Supervised Learning with MLlib – Classification, discusses supervised learning when the outcome variable is discrete.

Chapter 9, Unsupervised Learning with MLlib, covers unsupervised learning algorithms such as k-means.

Chapter 10, Recommender Systems, introduces building recommender systems using various techniques, such as ALS.

Chapter 11, Graph Processing Using GraphX, talks about various graph processing algorithms using GraphX.

Chapter 12, Optimizations and Performance Tuning, covers various optimizations on Apache Spark and performance tuning techniques.

What you need for this book

You need the InfoObjects Big Data Sandbox software to proceed with the examples in this book. This software can be downloaded from `http://www.infoobjects.com`.

Who this book is for

If you are a data engineer, an application developer, or a data scientist who would like to leverage the power of Apache Spark to get better insights from big data, then this is the book for you.

Sections

In this book, you will find several headings that appear frequently (Getting ready, How to do it, How it works, There's more, and See also).

To give clear instructions on how to complete a recipe, we use these sections as follows:

Getting ready

This section tells you what to expect in the recipe, and describes how to set up any software or any preliminary settings required for the recipe.

How to do it...

This section contains the steps required to follow the recipe.

How it works...

This section usually consists of a detailed explanation of what happened in the previous section.

There's more...

This section consists of additional information about the recipe in order to make the reader more knowledgeable about the recipe.

See also

This section provides helpful links to other useful information the recipe.

Conventions

In this book, you will find a number of text styles that distinguish between different kinds of information. Here are some examples of these styles and an explanation of their meaning.

Code words in text, database table names, folder names, filenames, file extensions, pathnames, dummy URLs, user input, and Twitter handles are shown as follows: "Spark expects Java to be installed and the `JAVA_HOME` environment variable to be set."

A block of code is set as follows:

```
lazy val root = (project in file("."))
  settings(
    name := "wordcount"
  )
```

Any command-line input or output is written as follows:

```
$ wget http://d3kbcqa49mib13.cloudfront.net/spark-1.4.0-bin-hadoop2.4.tgz
```

New terms and **important words** are shown in bold. Words that you see on the screen, for example, in menus or dialog boxes, appear in the text like this: "Click on **Security Credentials** under your account name in the top-right corner."

> Warnings or important notes appear in a box like this.

> Tips and tricks appear like this.

Reader feedback

Feedback from our readers is always welcome. Let us know what you think about this book—what you liked or disliked. Reader feedback is important for us as it helps us develop titles that you will really get the most out of.

To send us general feedback, simply e-mail `feedback@packtpub.com`, and mention the book's title in the subject of your message.

If there is a topic that you have expertise in and you are interested in either writing or contributing to a book, see our author guide at `www.packtpub.com/authors`.

Customer support

Now that you are the proud owner of a Packt book, we have a number of things to help you to get the most from your purchase.

Downloading the color images of this book

We also provide you with a PDF file that has color images of the screenshots/diagrams used in this book. The color images will help you better understand the changes in the output. You can download this file from: `https://www.packtpub.com/sites/default/files/downloads/70610S_ColorImages.pdf`.

Errata

Although we have taken every care to ensure the accuracy of our content, mistakes do happen. If you find a mistake in one of our books—maybe a mistake in the text or the code—we would be grateful if you could report this to us. By doing so, you can save other readers from frustration and help us improve subsequent versions of this book. If you find any errata, please report them by visiting `http://www.packtpub.com/submit-errata`, selecting your book, clicking on the **Errata Submission Form** link, and entering the details of your errata. Once your errata are verified, your submission will be accepted and the errata will be uploaded to our website or added to any list of existing errata under the Errata section of that title.

To view the previously submitted errata, go to `https://www.packtpub.com/books/content/support` and enter the name of the book in the search field. The required information will appear under the **Errata** section.

Piracy

Piracy of copyrighted material on the Internet is an ongoing problem across all media. At Packt, we take the protection of our copyright and licenses very seriously. If you come across any illegal copies of our works in any form on the Internet, please provide us with the location address or website name immediately so that we can pursue a remedy.

Please contact us at `copyright@packtpub.com` with a link to the suspected pirated material.

We appreciate your help in protecting our authors and our ability to bring you valuable content.

Questions

If you have a problem with any aspect of this book, you can contact us at `questions@packtpub.com`, and we will do our best to address the problem.

1

Getting Started with Apache Spark

In this chapter, we will set up Spark and configure it. This chapter is divided into the following recipes:

- Installing Spark from binaries
- Building the Spark source code with Maven
- Launching Spark on Amazon EC2
- Deploying Spark on a cluster in standalone mode
- Deploying Spark on a cluster with Mesos
- Deploying Spark on a cluster with YARN
- Using Tachyon as an off-heap storage layer

Introduction

Apache Spark is a general-purpose cluster computing system to process big data workloads. What sets Spark apart from its predecessors, such as MapReduce, is its speed, ease-of-use, and sophisticated analytics.

Apache Spark was originally developed at AMPLab, UC Berkeley, in 2009. It was made open source in 2010 under the BSD license and switched to the Apache 2.0 license in 2013. Toward the later part of 2013, the creators of Spark founded Databricks to focus on Spark's development and future releases.

Talking about speed, Spark can achieve sub-second latency on big data workloads. To achieve such low latency, Spark makes use of the memory for storage. In MapReduce, memory is primarily used for actual computation. Spark uses memory both to compute and store objects.

Spark also provides a unified runtime connecting to various big data storage sources, such as HDFS, Cassandra, HBase, and S3. It also provides a rich set of higher-level libraries for different big data compute tasks, such as machine learning, SQL processing, graph processing, and real-time streaming. These libraries make development faster and can be combined in an arbitrary fashion.

Though Spark is written in Scala, and this book only focuses on recipes in Scala, Spark also supports Java and Python.

Spark is an open source community project, and everyone uses the pure open source Apache distributions for deployments, unlike Hadoop, which has multiple distributions available with vendor enhancements.

The following figure shows the Spark ecosystem:

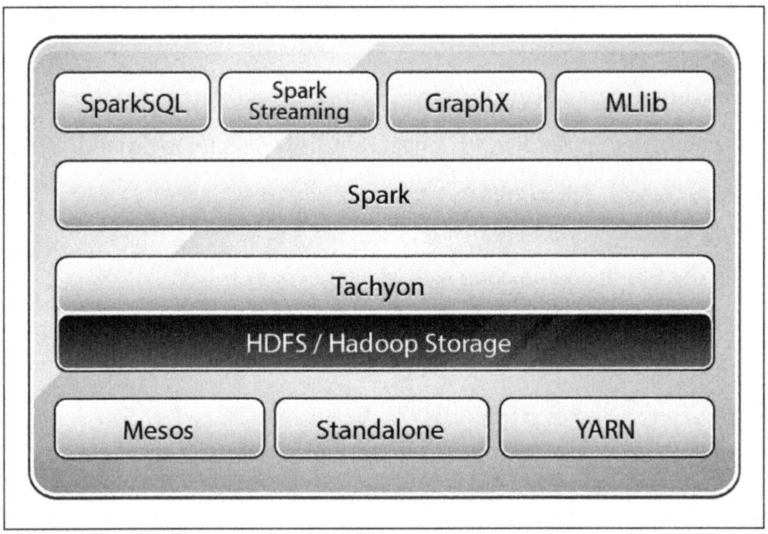

The Spark runtime runs on top of a variety of cluster managers, including YARN (Hadoop's compute framework), Mesos, and Spark's own cluster manager called **standalone mode**. Tachyon is a memory-centric distributed file system that enables reliable file sharing at memory speed across cluster frameworks. In short, it is an off-heap storage layer in memory, which helps share data across jobs and users. Mesos is a cluster manager, which is evolving into a data center operating system. YARN is Hadoop's compute framework that has a robust resource management feature that Spark can seamlessly use.

Installing Spark from binaries

Spark can be either built from the source code or precompiled binaries can be downloaded from `http://spark.apache.org`. For a standard use case, binaries are good enough, and this recipe will focus on installing Spark using binaries.

Getting ready

All the recipes in this book are developed using Ubuntu Linux but should work fine on any POSIX environment. Spark expects Java to be installed and the `JAVA_HOME` environment variable to be set.

In Linux/Unix systems, there are certain standards for the location of files and directories, which we are going to follow in this book. The following is a quick cheat sheet:

Directory	Description
`/bin`	Essential command binaries
`/etc`	Host-specific system configuration
`/opt`	Add-on application software packages
`/var`	Variable data
`/tmp`	Temporary files
`/home`	User home directories

How to do it...

At the time of writing this, Spark's current version is 1.4. Please check the latest version from Spark's download page at `http://spark.apache.org/downloads.html`. Binaries are developed with a most recent and stable version of Hadoop. To use a specific version of Hadoop, the recommended approach is to build from sources, which will be covered in the next recipe.

The following are the installation steps:

1. Open the terminal and download binaries using the following command:

   ```
   $ wget http://d3kbcqa49mib13.cloudfront.net/spark-1.4.0-bin-hadoop2.4.tgz
   ```

2. Unpack binaries:

   ```
   $ tar -zxf spark-1.4.0-bin-hadoop2.4.tgz
   ```

3. Rename the folder containing binaries by stripping the version information:

   $ sudo mv spark-1.4.0-bin-hadoop2.4 spark

4. Move the configuration folder to the `/etc` folder so that it can be made a symbolic link later:

   $ sudo mv spark/conf/* /etc/spark

5. Create your company-specific installation directory under `/opt`. As the recipes in this book are tested on `infoobjects` sandbox, we are going to use `infoobjects` as directory name. Create the `/opt/infoobjects` directory:

   $ sudo mkdir -p /opt/infoobjects

6. Move the `spark` directory to `/opt/infoobjects` as it's an add-on software package:

   $ sudo mv spark /opt/infoobjects/

7. Change the ownership of the `spark` home directory to `root`:

   $ sudo chown -R root:root /opt/infoobjects/spark

8. Change permissions of the `spark` home directory, `0755 = user:read-write-execute group:read-execute world:read-execute`:

   $ sudo chmod -R 755 /opt/infoobjects/spark

9. Move to the `spark` home directory:

   $ cd /opt/infoobjects/spark

10. Create the symbolic link:

    $ sudo ln -s /etc/spark conf

11. Append to `PATH` in `.bashrc`:

    $ echo "export PATH=$PATH:/opt/infoobjects/spark/bin" >> /home/hduser/.bashrc

12. Open a new terminal.
13. Create the `log` directory in `/var`:

    $ sudo mkdir -p /var/log/spark

14. Make `hduser` the owner of the Spark `log` directory.

    $ sudo chown -R hduser:hduser /var/log/spark

15. Create the Spark `tmp` directory:

    $ mkdir /tmp/spark

16. Configure Spark with the help of the following command lines:

```
$ cd /etc/spark
$ echo "export HADOOP_CONF_DIR=/opt/infoobjects/hadoop/etc/hadoop"
>> spark-env.sh
$ echo "export YARN_CONF_DIR=/opt/infoobjects/hadoop/etc/Hadoop"
>> spark-env.sh
$ echo "export SPARK_LOG_DIR=/var/log/spark" >> spark-env.sh
$ echo "export SPARK_WORKER_DIR=/tmp/spark" >> spark-env.sh
```

Building the Spark source code with Maven

Installing Spark using binaries works fine in most cases. For advanced cases, such as the following (but not limited to), compiling from the source code is a better option:

- Compiling for a specific Hadoop version
- Adding the Hive integration
- Adding the YARN integration

Getting ready

The following are the prerequisites for this recipe to work:

- Java 1.6 or a later version
- Maven 3.x

How to do it...

The following are the steps to build the Spark source code with Maven:

1. Increase `MaxPermSize` for heap:

```
$ echo "export _JAVA_OPTIONS=\"-XX:MaxPermSize=1G\""  >> /home/
hduser/.bashrc
```

2. Open a new terminal window and download the Spark source code from GitHub:

```
$ wget https://github.com/apache/spark/archive/branch-1.4.zip
```

3. Unpack the archive:

```
$ gunzip branch-1.4.zip
```

4. Move to the `spark` directory:

```
$ cd spark
```

5. Compile the sources with these flags: Yarn enabled, Hadoop version 2.4, Hive enabled, and skipping tests for faster compilation:

   ```
   $ mvn -Pyarn -Phadoop-2.4 -Dhadoop.version=2.4.0 -Phive
   -DskipTests clean package
   ```

6. Move the `conf` folder to the `etc` folder so that it can be made a symbolic link:

   ```
   $ sudo mv spark/conf /etc/
   ```

7. Move the `spark` directory to `/opt` as it's an add-on software package:

   ```
   $ sudo mv spark /opt/infoobjects/spark
   ```

8. Change the ownership of the `spark` home directory to `root`:

   ```
   $ sudo chown -R root:root /opt/infoobjects/spark
   ```

9. Change the permissions of the `spark` home directory `0755 = user:rwx group:r-x world:r-x`:

   ```
   $ sudo chmod -R 755 /opt/infoobjects/spark
   ```

10. Move to the `spark` home directory:

    ```
    $ cd /opt/infoobjects/spark
    ```

11. Create a symbolic link:

    ```
    $ sudo ln -s /etc/spark conf
    ```

12. Put the Spark executable in the path by editing `.bashrc`:

    ```
    $ echo "export PATH=$PATH:/opt/infoobjects/spark/bin" >> /home/
    hduser/.bashrc
    ```

13. Create the `log` directory in `/var`:

    ```
    $ sudo mkdir -p /var/log/spark
    ```

14. Make `hduser` the owner of the Spark `log` directory:

    ```
    $ sudo chown -R hduser:hduser /var/log/spark
    ```

15. Create the Spark `tmp` directory:

    ```
    $ mkdir /tmp/spark
    ```

16. Configure Spark with the help of the following command lines:

    ```
    $ cd /etc/spark
    $ echo "export HADOOP_CONF_DIR=/opt/infoobjects/hadoop/etc/hadoop"
    >> spark-env.sh
    $ echo "export YARN_CONF_DIR=/opt/infoobjects/hadoop/etc/Hadoop"
    >> spark-env.sh
    $ echo "export SPARK_LOG_DIR=/var/log/spark" >> spark-env.sh
    $ echo "export SPARK_WORKER_DIR=/tmp/spark" >> spark-env.sh
    ```

Launching Spark on Amazon EC2

Amazon Elastic Compute Cloud (**Amazon EC2**) is a web service that provides resizable compute instances in the cloud. Amazon EC2 provides the following features:

- On-demand delivery of IT resources via the Internet
- The provision of as many instances as you like
- Payment for the hours you use instances like your utility bill
- No setup cost, no installation, and no overhead at all
- When you no longer need instances, you either shut down or terminate and walk away
- The availability of these instances on all familiar operating systems

EC2 provides different types of instances to meet all compute needs, such as general-purpose instances, micro instances, memory-optimized instances, storage-optimized instances, and others. They have a free tier of micro-instances to try.

Getting ready

The `spark-ec2` script comes bundled with Spark and makes it easy to launch, manage, and shut down clusters on Amazon EC2.

Before you start, you need to do the following things:

1. Log in to the Amazon AWS account (`http://aws.amazon.com`).
2. Click on **Security Credentials** under your account name in the top-right corner.
3. Click on **Access Keys** and **Create New Access Key**:

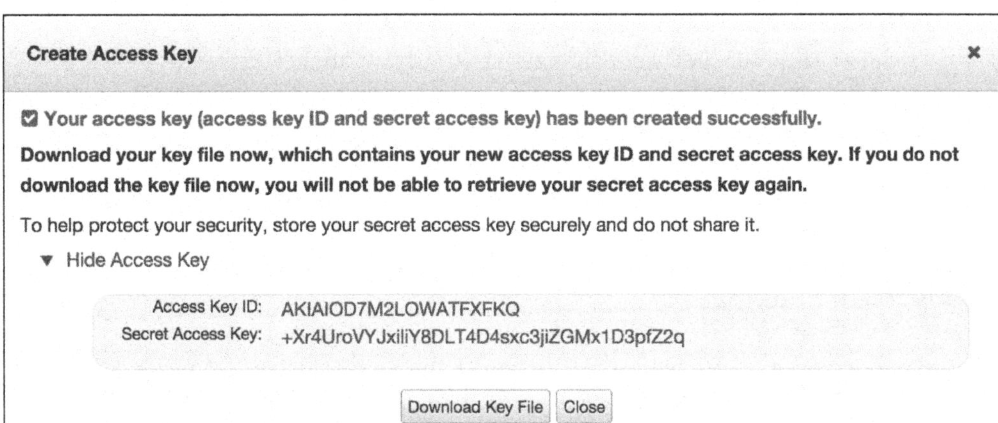

4. Note down the access key ID and secret access key.
5. Now go to **Services** | **EC2**.

6. Click on **Key Pairs** in left-hand menu under NETWORK & SECURITY.
7. Click on **Create Key Pair** and enter `kp-spark` as key-pair name:

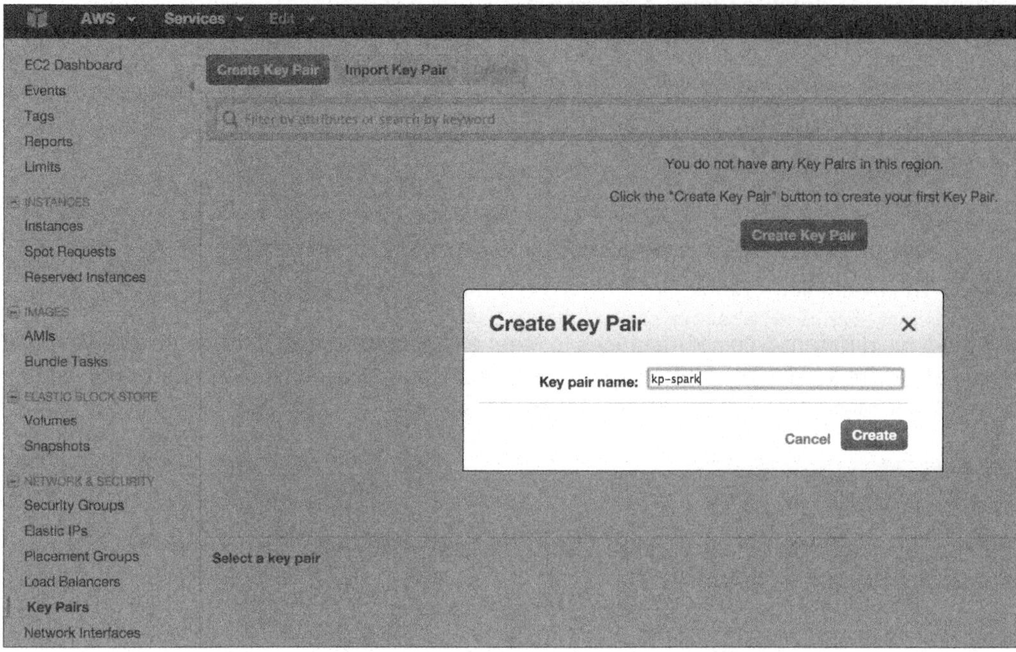

8. Download the private key file and copy it in the `/home/hduser/keypairs folder`.
9. Set permissions on key file to `600`.
10. Set environment variables to reflect access key ID and secret access key (please replace sample values with your own values):

```
$ echo "export AWS_ACCESS_KEY_ID=\"AKIAOD7M2LOWATFXFKQ\"" >> /
home/hduser/.bashrc
```

```
$ echo "export AWS_SECRET_ACCESS_KEY=\"+Xr4UroVYJxiLiY8DLT4DLT4D4s
xc3ijZGMx1D3pfZ2q\"" >> /home/hduser/.bashrc
```

```
$ echo "export PATH=$PATH:/opt/infoobjects/spark/ec2" >> /home/
hduser/.bashrc
```

How to do it...

1. Spark comes bundled with scripts to launch the Spark cluster on Amazon EC2. Let's launch the cluster using the following command:

```
$ cd /home/hduser
```

```
$ spark-ec2 -k <key-pair> -i <key-file> -s <num-slaves> launch
<cluster-name>
```

2. Launch the cluster with the example value:

```
$ spark-ec2 -k kp-spark -i /home/hduser/keypairs/kp-spark.pem
--hadoop-major-version 2  -s 3 launch spark-cluster
```

> - `<key-pair>`: This is the name of EC2 key-pair created in AWS
> - `<key-file>`: This is the private key file you downloaded
> - `<num-slaves>`: This is the number of slave nodes to launch
> - `<cluster-name>`: This is the name of the cluster

3. Sometimes, the default availability zones are not available; in that case, retry sending the request by specifying the specific availability zone you are requesting:

```
$ spark-ec2 -k kp-spark -i /home/hduser/keypairs/kp-spark.pem -z
us-east-1b --hadoop-major-version 2  -s 3 launch spark-cluster
```

4. If your application needs to retain data after the instance shuts down, attach EBS volume to it (for example, a 10 GB space):

```
$ spark-ec2 -k kp-spark -i /home/hduser/keypairs/kp-spark.pem
--hadoop-major-version 2 -ebs-vol-size 10 -s 3 launch spark-
cluster
```

5. If you use Amazon spot instances, here's the way to do it:

```
$ spark-ec2 -k kp-spark -i /home/hduser/keypairs/kp-spark.pem
-spot-price=0.15 --hadoop-major-version 2  -s 3 launch spark-
cluster
```

> Spot instances allow you to name your own price for Amazon EC2 computing capacity. You simply bid on spare Amazon EC2 instances and run them whenever your bid exceeds the current spot price, which varies in real-time based on supply and demand (source: `amazon.com`).

6. After everything is launched, check the status of the cluster by going to the web UI URL that will be printed at the end.

7. Check the status of the cluster:

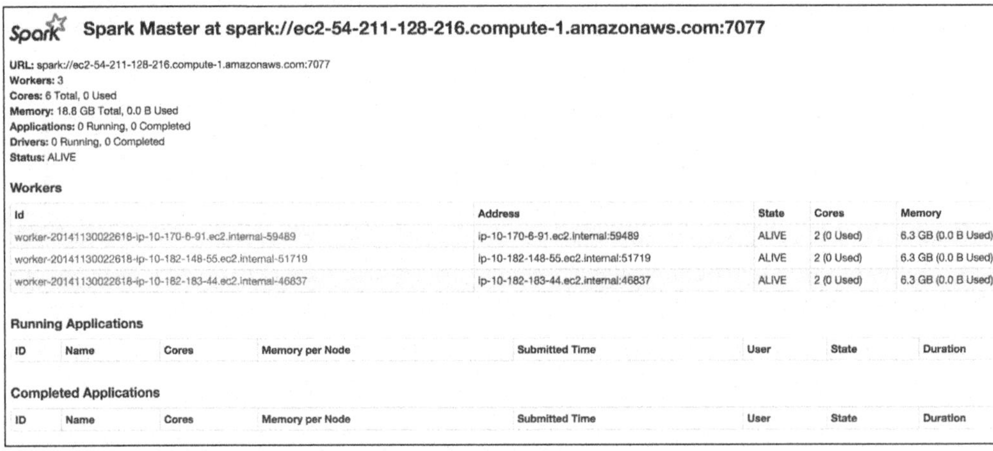

8. Now, to access the Spark cluster on EC2, let's connect to the master node using **secure shell protocol** (**SSH**):

```
$ spark-ec2 -k kp-spark -i /home/hduser/kp/kp-spark.pem  login
spark-cluster
```

You should get something like the following:

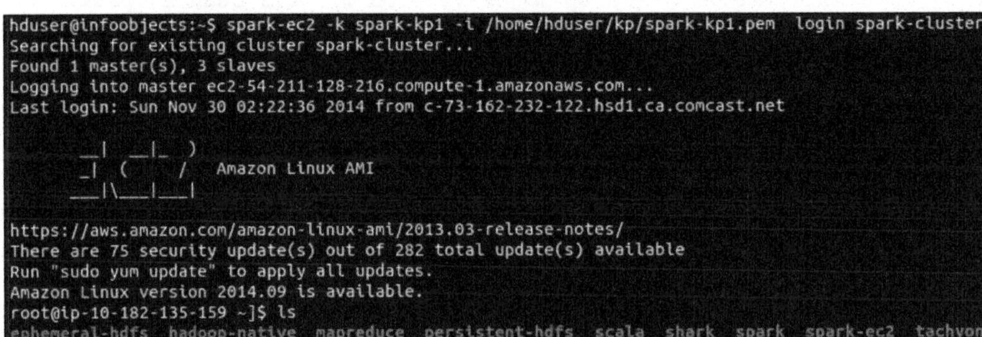

9. Check directories in the master node and see what they do:

Directory	Description
`ephemeral-hdfs`	This is the Hadoop instance for which data is ephemeral and gets deleted when you stop or restart the machine.
`persistent-hdfs`	Each node has a very small amount of persistent storage (approximately 3 GB). If you use this instance, data will be retained in that space.
`hadoop-native`	These are native libraries to support Hadoop, such as snappy compression libraries.

Directory	Description
Scala	This is Scala installation.
shark	This is Shark installation (Shark is no longer supported and is replaced by Spark SQL).
spark	This is Spark installation
spark-ec2	These are files to support this cluster deployment.
tachyon	This is Tachyon installation

10. Check the HDFS version in an ephemeral instance:

```
$ ephemeral-hdfs/bin/hadoop version
Hadoop 2.0.0-chd4.2.0
```

11. Check the HDFS version in persistent instance with the following command:

```
$ persistent-hdfs/bin/hadoop version
Hadoop 2.0.0-chd4.2.0
```

12. Change the configuration level in logs:

```
$ cd spark/conf
```

13. The default log level information is too verbose, so let's change it to Error:

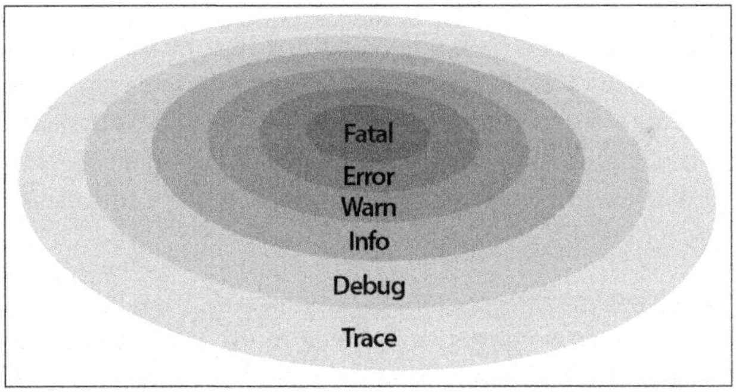

    1. Create the `log4.properties` file by renaming the template:

    ```
    $ mv log4j.properties.template log4j.properties
    ```

    2. Open `log4j.properties` in vi or your favorite editor:

    ```
    $ vi log4j.properties
    ```

    3. Change second line from `| log4j.rootCategory=INFO, console` to `| log4j.rootCategory=ERROR, console`.

14. Copy the configuration to all slave nodes after the change:

```
$ spark-ec2/copydir spark/conf
```

You should get something like this:

```
root@ip-10-168-32-181 ~]$ spark-ec2/copy-dir spark/conf/
RSYNC'ing /root/spark/conf to slaves...
ec2-174-129-51-11.compute-1.amazonaws.com
ec2-107-20-52-62.compute-1.amazonaws.com
ec2-54-224-17-251.compute-1.amazonaws.com
```

15. Destroy the Spark cluster:

    `$ spark-ec2 destroy spark-cluster`

See also

- `http://aws.amazon.com/ec2`

Deploying on a cluster in standalone mode

Compute resources in a distributed environment need to be managed so that resource utilization is efficient and every job gets a fair chance to run. Spark comes along with its own cluster manager conveniently called **standalone mode**. Spark also supports working with YARN and Mesos cluster managers.

The cluster manager that should be chosen is mostly driven by both legacy concerns and whether other frameworks, such as MapReduce, are sharing the same compute resource pool. If your cluster has legacy MapReduce jobs running, and all of them cannot be converted to Spark jobs, it is a good idea to use YARN as the cluster manager. Mesos is emerging as a data center operating system to conveniently manage jobs across frameworks, and is very compatible with Spark.

If the Spark framework is the only framework in your cluster, then standalone mode is good enough. As Spark evolves as technology, you will see more and more use cases of Spark being used as the standalone framework serving all big data compute needs. For example, some jobs may be using Apache Mahout at present because MLlib does not have a specific machine-learning library, which the job needs. As soon as MLlib gets this library, this particular job can be moved to Spark.

Getting ready

Let's consider a cluster of six nodes as an example setup: one master and five slaves (replace them with actual node names in your cluster):

`Master`

`m1.zettabytes.com`

`Slaves`

```
s1.zettabytes.com
s2.zettabytes.com
s3.zettabytes.com
s4.zettabytes.com
s5.zettabytes.com
```

How to do it...

1. Since Spark's standalone mode is the default, all you need to do is to have Spark binaries installed on both master and slave machines. Put `/opt/infoobjects/spark/sbin` in path on every node:

   ```
   $ echo "export PATH=$PATH:/opt/infoobjects/spark/sbin" >> /home/hduser/.bashrc
   ```

2. Start the standalone master server (SSH to master first):

   ```
   hduser@m1.zettabytes.com~] start-master.sh
   ```

   Master, by default, starts on port 7077, which slaves use to connect to it. It also has a web UI at port 8088.

3. Please SSH to master node and start slaves:

   ```
   hduser@s1.zettabytes.com~] spark-class org.apache.spark.deploy.worker.Worker spark://m1.zettabytes.com:7077
   ```

Argument (for fine-grained configuration, the following parameters work with both master and slaves)	**Meaning**
`-i <ipaddress>,-ip <ipaddress>`	IP address/DNS service listens on
`-p <port>, --port <port>`	Port service listens on
`--webui-port <port>`	Port for web UI (by default, 8080 for master and 8081 for worker)
`-c <cores>,--cores <cores>`	Total CPU cores Spark applications that can be used on a machine (worker only)
`-m <memory>,--memory <memory>`	Total RAM Spark applications that can be used on a machine (worker only)
`-d <dir>,--work-dir <dir>`	The directory to use for scratch space and job output logs

4. Rather than manually starting master and slave daemons on each node, it can also be accomplished using cluster launch scripts.

5. First, create the `conf/slaves` file on a master node and add one line per slave hostname (using an example of five slaves nodes, replace with the DNS of slave nodes in your cluster):

```
hduser@m1.zettabytes.com~] echo "s1.zettabytes.com" >> conf/slaves
hduser@m1.zettabytes.com~] echo "s2.zettabytes.com" >> conf/slaves
hduser@m1.zettabytes.com~] echo "s3.zettabytes.com" >> conf/slaves
hduser@m1.zettabytes.com~] echo "s4.zettabytes.com" >> conf/slaves
hduser@m1.zettabytes.com~] echo "s5.zettabytes.com" >> conf/slaves
```

Once the slave machine is set up, you can call the following scripts to start/stop cluster:

Script name	Purpose
`start-master.sh`	Starts a master instance on the host machine
`start-slaves.sh`	Starts a slave instance on each node in the slaves file
`start-all.sh`	Starts both master and slaves
`stop-master.sh`	Stops the master instance on the host machine
`stop-slaves.sh`	Stops the slave instance on all nodes in the slaves file
`stop-all.sh`	Stops both master and slaves

6. Connect an application to the cluster through the Scala code:

```
val sparkContext = new SparkContext(new SparkConf().
setMaster("spark://m1.zettabytes.com:7077")
```

7. Connect to the cluster through Spark shell:

```
$ spark-shell --master spark://master:7077
```

How it works...

In standalone mode, Spark follows the master slave architecture, very much like Hadoop, MapReduce, and YARN. The compute master daemon is called **Spark master** and runs on one master node. Spark master can be made highly available using ZooKeeper. You can also add more standby masters on the fly, if needed.

The compute slave daemon is called **worker** and is on each slave node. The worker daemon does the following:

- Reports the availability of compute resources on a slave node, such as the number of cores, memory, and others, to Spark master
- Spawns the executor when asked to do so by Spark master
- Restarts the executor if it dies

There is, at most, one executor per application per slave machine.

Both Spark master and worker are very lightweight. Typically, memory allocation between 500 MB to 1 GB is sufficient. This value can be set in `conf/spark-env.sh` by setting the `SPARK_DAEMON_MEMORY` parameter. For example, the following configuration will set the memory to 1 gigabits for both master and worker daemon. Make sure you have `sudo` as the super user before running it:

```
$ echo "export SPARK_DAEMON_MEMORY=1g" >> /opt/infoobjects/spark/conf/
spark-env.sh
```

By default, each slave node has one worker instance running on it. Sometimes, you may have a few machines that are more powerful than others. In that case, you can spawn more than one worker on that machine by the following configuration (only on those machines):

```
$ echo "export SPARK_WORKER_INSTANCES=2" >> /opt/infoobjects/spark/conf/
spark-env.sh
```

Spark worker, by default, uses all cores on the slave machine for its executors. If you would like to limit the number of cores the worker can use, you can set it to that number (for example, 12) by the following configuration:

```
$ echo "export SPARK_WORKER_CORES=12" >> /opt/infoobjects/spark/conf/
spark-env.sh
```

Spark worker, by default, uses all the available RAM (1 GB for executors). Note that you cannot allocate how much memory each specific executor will use (you can control this from the driver configuration). To assign another value for the total memory (for example, 24 GB) to be used by all executors combined, execute the following setting:

```
$ echo "export SPARK_WORKER_MEMORY=24g" >> /opt/infoobjects/spark/conf/
spark-env.sh
```

There are some settings you can do at the driver level:

- To specify the maximum number of CPU cores to be used by a given application across the cluster, you can set the `spark.cores.max` configuration in Spark submit or Spark shell as follows:

  ```
  $ spark-submit --conf spark.cores.max=12
  ```

- To specify the amount of memory each executor should be allocated (the minimum recommendation is 8 GB), you can set the `spark.executor.memory` configuration in Spark submit or Spark shell as follows:

  ```
  $ spark-submit --conf spark.executor.memory=8g
  ```

The following diagram depicts the high-level architecture of a Spark cluster:

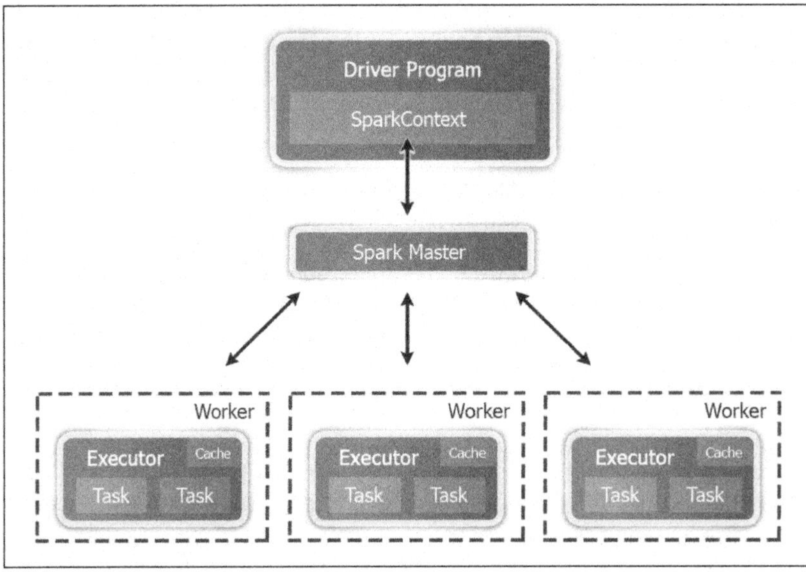

See also

- `http://spark.apache.org/docs/latest/spark-standalone.html` to find more configuration options

Deploying on a cluster with Mesos

Mesos is slowly emerging as a data center operating system to manage all compute resources across a data center. Mesos runs on any computer running the Linux operating system. Mesos is built using the same principles as Linux kernel. Let's see how we can install Mesos.

How to do it...

Mesosphere provides a binary distribution of Mesos. The most recent package for the Mesos distribution can be installed from the Mesosphere repositories by performing the following steps:

1. Execute Mesos on Ubuntu OS with the trusty version:

```
$ sudo apt-key adv --keyserver keyserver.ubuntu.com --recv
E56151BF DISTRO=$(lsb_release -is | tr '[:upper:]' '[:lower:]')
CODENAME=$(lsb_release -cs)
```

```
$ sudo vi /etc/apt/sources.list.d/mesosphere.list

deb http://repos.mesosphere.io/Ubuntu trusty main
```

2. Update the repositories:

   ```
   $ sudo apt-get -y update
   ```

3. Install Mesos:

   ```
   $ sudo apt-get -y install mesos
   ```

4. To connect Spark to Mesos to integrate Spark with Mesos, make Spark binaries available to Mesos and configure the Spark driver to connect to Mesos.
5. Use Spark binaries from the first recipe and upload to HDFS:

   ```
   $ hdfs dfs -put spark-1.4.0-bin-hadoop2.4.tgz spark-1.4.0-bin-hadoop2.4.tgz
   ```

6. The master URL for single master Mesos is `mesos://host:5050`, and for the ZooKeeper managed Mesos cluster, it is `mesos://zk://host:2181`.
7. Set the following variables in `spark-env.sh`:

   ```
   $ sudo vi spark-env.sh
   export MESOS_NATIVE_LIBRARY=/usr/local/lib/libmesos.so
   export SPARK_EXECUTOR_URI= hdfs://localhost:9000/user/hduser/spark-1.4.0-bin-hadoop2.4.tgz
   ```

8. Run from the Scala program:

   ```
   val conf = new SparkConf().setMaster("mesos://host:5050")
   val sparkContext = new SparkContext(conf)
   ```

9. Run from the Spark shell:

   ```
   $ spark-shell --master mesos://host:5050
   ```

> Mesos has two run modes:
>
> **Fine-grained**: In fine-grained (default) mode, every Spark task runs as a separate Mesos task
>
> **Coarse-grained**: This mode will launch only one long-running Spark task on each Mesos machine

10. To run in the coarse-grained mode, set the `spark.mesos.coarse` property:

    ```
    conf.set("spark.mesos.coarse","true")
    ```

Deploying on a cluster with YARN

Yet another resource negotiator (**YARN**) is Hadoop's compute framework that runs on top of HDFS, which is Hadoop's storage layer.

YARN follows the master slave architecture. The master daemon is called `ResourceManager` and the slave daemon is called `NodeManager`. Besides this application, life cycle management is done by `ApplicationMaster`, which can be spawned on any slave node and is alive for the lifetime of an application.

When Spark is run on YARN, `ResourceManager` performs the role of Spark master and `NodeManagers` work as executor nodes.

While running Spark with YARN, each Spark executor is run as YARN container.

Getting ready

Running Spark on YARN requires a binary distribution of Spark that has YARN support. In both Spark installation recipes, we have taken care of it.

How to do it...

1. To run Spark on YARN, the first step is to set the configuration:

   ```
   HADOOP_CONF_DIR: to write to HDFS
   YARN_CONF_DIR: to connect to YARN ResourceManager
   $ cd /opt/infoobjects/spark/conf (or /etc/spark)
   $ sudo vi spark-env.sh
   export HADOOP_CONF_DIR=/opt/infoobjects/hadoop/etc/Hadoop
   export YARN_CONF_DIR=/opt/infoobjects/hadoop/etc/hadoop
   ```

You can see this in the following screenshot:

```
#!/usr/bin/env bash

# This file contains environment variables required to run Spark. Copy it as
# spark-env.sh and edit that to configure Spark for your site.
#
# The following variables can be set in this file:
# - SPARK_LOCAL_IP, to set the IP address Spark binds to on this node
# - MESOS_NATIVE_LIBRARY, to point to your libmesos.so if you use Mesos
# - SPARK_JAVA_OPTS, to set node-specific JVM options for Spark. Note that
#   we recommend setting app-wide options in the application's driver program.
#     Examples of node-specific options : -Dspark.local.dir, GC options
#     Examples of app-wide options : -Dspark.serializer
#
# If using the standalone deploy mode, you can also set variables for it here:
# - SPARK_MASTER_IP, to bind the master to a different IP address or hostname
# - SPARK_MASTER_PORT / SPARK_MASTER_WEBUI_PORT, to use non-default ports
# - SPARK_WORKER_CORES, to set the number of cores to use on this machine
# - SPARK_WORKER_MEMORY, to set how much memory to use (e.g. 1000m, 2g)
# - SPARK_WORKER_PORT / SPARK_WORKER_WEBUI_PORT
# - SPARK_WORKER_INSTANCES, to set the number of worker processes per node
# - SPARK_WORKER_DIR, to set the working directory of worker processes
export HADOOP_CONF_DIR=/opt/infoobjects/hadoop/etc/hadoop
export YARN_CONF_DIR=/opt/infoobjects/hadoop/etc/hadoop
export SPARK_LOG_DIR=/var/log/spark
export SPARK_WORKER_DIR=/var/spark/worker
```

2. The following command launches YARN Spark in the `yarn-client` mode:

   ```
   $ spark-submit --class path.to.your.Class --master yarn-client
   [options] <app jar> [app options]
   ```

   Here's an example:

   ```
   $ spark-submit --class com.infoobjects.TwitterFireHose --master
   yarn-client --num-executors 3 --driver-memory 4g --executor-memory
   2g --executor-cores 1 target/sparkio.jar 10
   ```

3. The following command launches Spark shell in the `yarn-client` mode:

   ```
   $ spark-shell --master yarn-client
   ```

4. The command to launch in the `yarn-cluster` mode is as follows:

   ```
   $ spark-submit --class path.to.your.Class --master yarn-cluster
   [options] <app jar> [app options]
   ```

   Here's an example:

   ```
   $ spark-submit --class com.infoobjects.TwitterFireHose --master
   yarn-cluster --num-executors 3 --driver-memory 4g --executor-
   memory 2g --executor-cores 1 target/sparkio.jar 10
   ```

How it works...

Spark applications on YARN run in two modes:

- `yarn-client`: Spark Driver runs in the client process outside of YARN cluster, and `ApplicationMaster` is only used to negotiate resources from ResourceManager
- `yarn-cluster`: Spark Driver runs in `ApplicationMaster` spawned by `NodeManager` on a slave node

The `yarn-cluster` mode is recommended for production deployments, while the `yarn-client` mode is good for development and debugging when you would like to see immediate output. There is no need to specify Spark master in either mode as it's picked from the Hadoop configuration, and the master parameter is either `yarn-client` or `yarn-cluster`.

The following figure shows how Spark is run with YARN in the client mode:

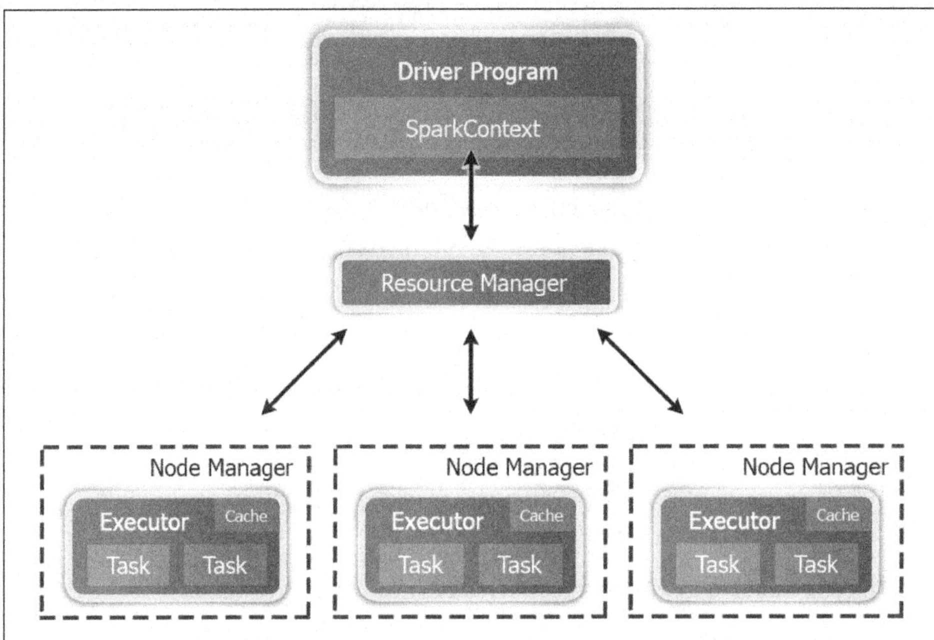

The following figure shows how Spark is run with YARN in the cluster mode:

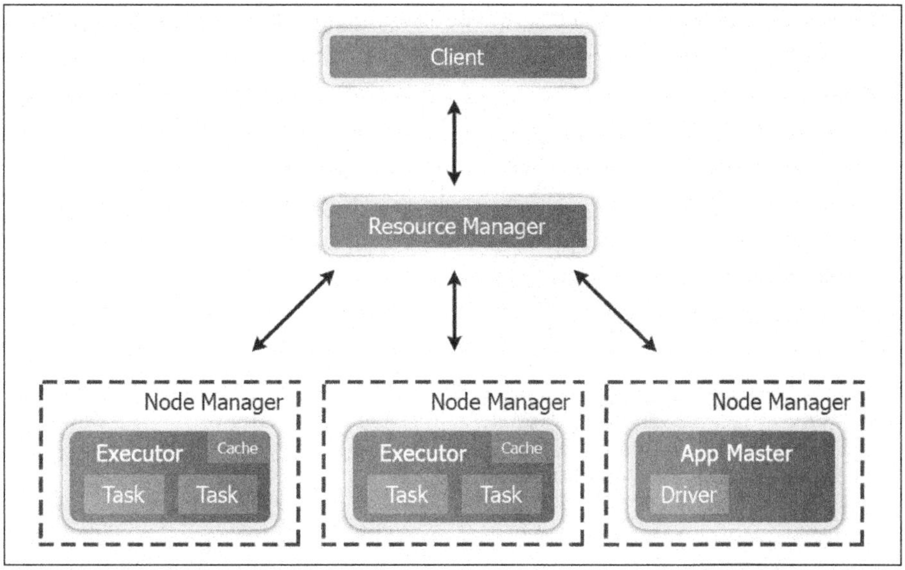

In the YARN mode, the following configuration parameters can be set:

- `--num-executors`: Configure how many executors will be allocated
- `--executor-memory`: RAM per executor
- `--executor-cores`: CPU cores per executor

Using Tachyon as an off-heap storage layer

Spark RDDs are a great way to store datasets in memory while ending up with multiple copies of the same data in different applications. Tachyon solves some of the challenges with Spark RDD management. A few of them are:

- RDD only exists for the duration of the Spark application
- The same process performs the compute and RDD in-memory storage; so, if a process crashes, in-memory storage also goes away
- Different jobs cannot share an RDD even if they are for the same underlying data, for example, an HDFS block that leads to:
    - Slow writes to disk
    - Duplication of data in memory, higher memory footprint
- If the output of one application needs to be shared with the other application, it's slow due to the replication in the disk

Tachyon provides an off-heap memory layer to solve these problems. This layer, being off-heap, is immune to process crashes and is also not subject to garbage collection. This also lets RDDs be shared across applications and outlive a specific job or session; in essence, one single copy of data resides in memory, as shown in the following figure:

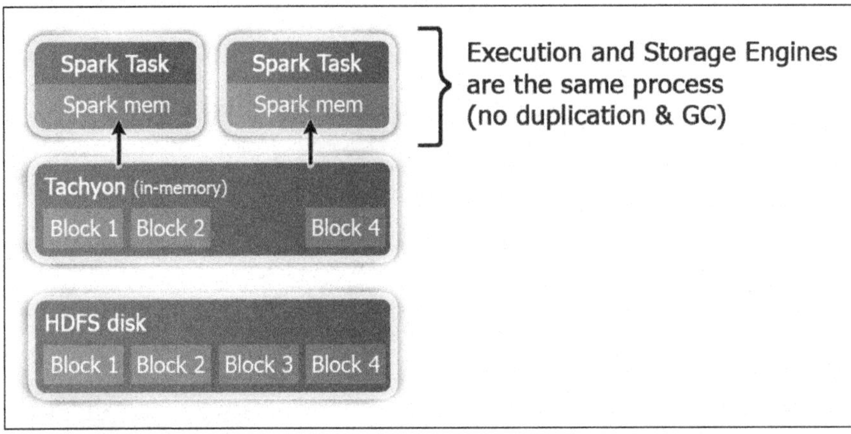

How to do it...

1. Let's download and compile Tachyon (Tachyon, by default, comes configured for Hadoop 1.0.4, so it needs to be compiled from sources for the right Hadoop version). Replace the version with the current version. The current version at the time of writing this book is 0.6.4:

```
$ wget https://github.com/amplab/tachyon/archive/v<version>.zip
```

2. Unarchive the source code:

```
$ unzip  v-<version>.zip
```

3. Remove the version from the `tachyon` source folder name for convenience:

```
$ mv tachyon-<version> tachyon
```

4. Change the directory to the `tachyon` folder:

```
$ cd tachyon
$ mvn -Dhadoop.version=2.4.0 clean package -DskipTests=true
$ cd conf
$ sudo mkdir -p /var/tachyon/journal
$ sudo chown -R hduser:hduser /var/tachyon/journal
```

```
$ sudo mkdir -p /var/tachyon/ramdisk
$ sudo chown -R hduser:hduser /var/tachyon/ramdisk

$ mv tachyon-env.sh.template tachyon-env.sh
$ vi tachyon-env.sh
```

5. Comment the following line:

```
export TACHYON_UNDERFS_ADDRESS=$TACHYON_HOME/underfs
```

6. Uncomment the following line:

```
export TACHYON_UNDERFS_ADDRESS=hdfs://localhost:9000
```

7. Change the following properties:

```
-Dtachyon.master.journal.folder=/var/tachyon/journal/

export TACHYON_RAM_FOLDER=/var/tachyon/ramdisk

$ sudo mkdir -p /var/log/tachyon
$ sudo chown -R hduser:hduser /var/log/tachyon
$ vi log4j.properties
```

8. Replace `${tachyon.home}` with `/var/log/tachyon`.
9. Create a new `core-site.xml` file in the `conf` directory:

```
$ sudo vi core-site.xml
<configuration>
<property>
    <name>fs.tachyon.impl</name>
    <value>tachyon.hadoop.TFS</value>
  </property>
</configuration>
$ cd ~
$ sudo mv tachyon /opt/infoobjects/
$ sudo chown -R root:root /opt/infoobjects/tachyon
$ sudo chmod -R 755 /opt/infoobjects/tachyon
```

10. Add `<tachyon home>/bin` to the path:

```
$ echo "export PATH=$PATH:/opt/infoobjects/tachyon/bin" >> /home/
hduser/.bashrc
```

11. Restart the shell and format Tachyon:

    $ tachyon format

    $ tachyon-start.sh local //you need to enter root password as RamFS needs to be formatted

    Tachyon's web interface is `http://hostname:19999`:

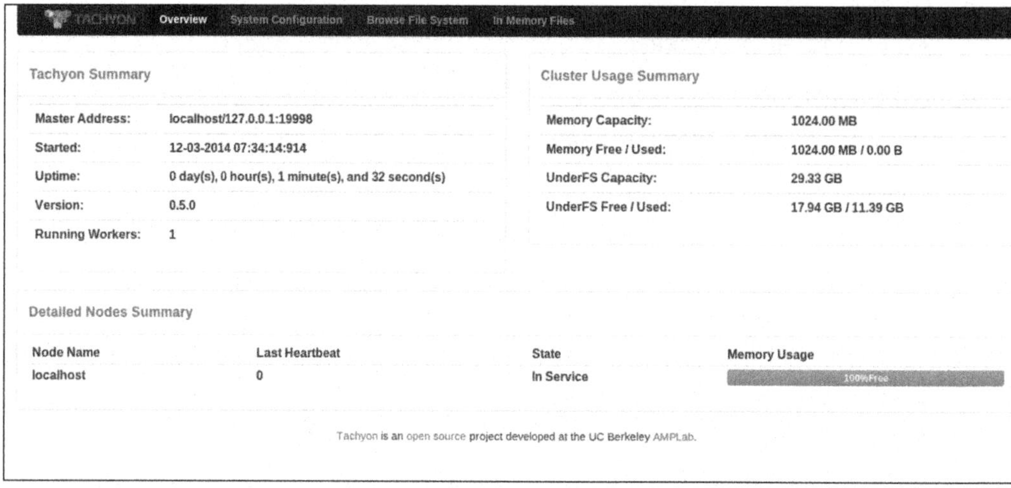

12. Run the sample program to see whether Tachyon is running fine:

    $ tachyon runTest Basic CACHE_THROUGH

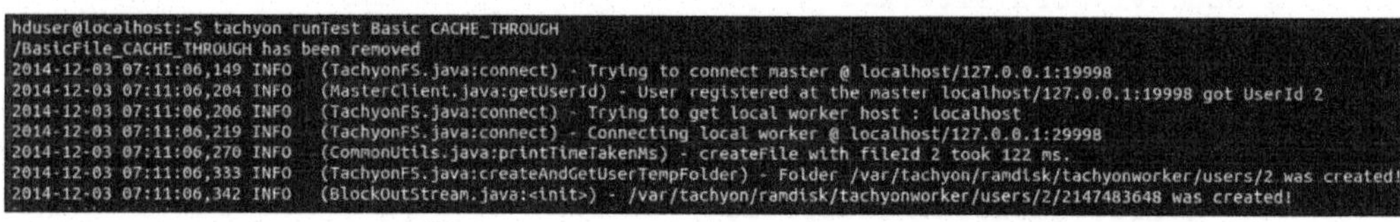

13. You can stop Tachyon any time by running the following command:

    $ tachyon-stop.sh

14. Run Spark on Tachyon:

```
$ spark-shell
scala> val words = sc.textFile("tachyon://localhost:19998/words")
scala> words.count
scala> words.saveAsTextFile("tachyon://localhost:19998/w2")
scala> val person = sc.textFile("hdfs://localhost:9000/user/
hduser/person")
scala> import org.apache.spark.api.java._
scala> person.persist(StorageLevels.OFF_HEAP)
```

See also

- `http://www.cs.berkeley.edu/~haoyuan/papers/2013_ladis_tachyon.pdf` to learn about the origins of Tachyon
- `http://www.tachyonnexus.com`

2
Developing Applications with Spark

In this chapter, we will cover:

- Exploring the Spark shell
- Developing a Spark application in Eclipse with Maven
- Developing Spark applications in Eclipse with SBT
- Developing a Spark application in Intellij IDEA with Maven
- Developing a Spark application in Intellij IDEA with SBT

Introduction

To create production quality Spark jobs/application, it is useful to use various **integrated development environments** (**IDEs**) and build tools. This chapter will cover various IDEs and build tools.

Exploring the Spark shell

Spark comes bundled with a REPL shell, which is a wrapper around the Scala shell. Though the Spark shell looks like a command line for simple things, in reality a lot of complex queries can also be executed using it. This chapter explores different development environments in which Spark applications can be developed.

How to do it...

Hadoop MapReduce's word count becomes very simple with the Spark shell. In this recipe, we are going to create a simple 1-line text file, upload it to the **Hadoop distributed file system** (**HDFS**), and use Spark to count occurrences of words. Let's see how:

1. Create the `words` directory by using the following command:

   ```
   $ mkdir words
   ```

2. Get into the `words` directory:

   ```
   $ cd words
   ```

3. Create a `sh.txt` text file and enter `"to be or not to be"` in it:

   ```
   $ echo "to be or not to be" > sh.txt
   ```

4. Start the Spark shell:

   ```
   $ spark-shell
   ```

5. Load the `words` directory as RDD:

   ```
   Scala> val words = sc.textFile("hdfs://localhost:9000/user/hduser/
   words")
   ```

6. Count the number of lines (result: 1):

   ```
   Scala> words.count
   ```

7. Divide the line (or lines) into multiple words:

   ```
   Scala> val wordsFlatMap = words.flatMap(_.split("\\W+"))
   ```

8. Convert `word` to (word,1)—that is, output `1` as the value for each occurrence of `word` as a key:

   ```
   Scala> val wordsMap = wordsFlatMap.map( w => (w,1))
   ```

9. Use the `reduceByKey` method to add the number of occurrences for each word as a key (the function works on two consecutive values at a time represented by `a` and `b`):

   ```
   Scala> val wordCount = wordsMap.reduceByKey( (a,b) => (a+b))
   ```

10. Sort the results:

    ```
    Scala> val wordCountSorted = wordCount.sortByKey(true)
    ```

11. Print the RDD:

    ```
    Scala> wordCountSorted.collect.foreach(println)
    ```

12. Doing all of the preceding operations in one step is as follows:

    ```
    Scala> sc.textFile("hdfs://localhost:9000/user/hduser/words").
    flatMap(_.split("\\W+")).map( w => (w,1)). reduceByKey( (a,b) =>
    (a+b)).sortByKey(true).collect.foreach(println)
    ```

This gives us the following output:

```
(or,1)
(to,2)
(not,1)
(be,2)
```

Now you understand the basics, load HDFS with a large amount of text—for example, stories—and see the magic.

If you have the files in a compressed format, you can load them as is in HDFS. Both Hadoop and Spark have codecs for unzipping, which they use based on file extensions.

When `wordsFlatMap` was converted to `wordsMap` RDD, there was an implicit conversion. This converts RDD into `PairRDD`. This is an implicit conversion, which does not require anything to be done. If you are doing it in Scala code, please add the following `import` statement:

```
import org.apache.spark.SparkContext._
```

Developing Spark applications in Eclipse with Maven

Maven as a build tool has become the de-facto standard over the years. It's not surprising if we look little deeper into the promise Maven brings. Maven has two primary features and they are:

- **Convention over configuration**: Build tools prior to Maven gave developers freedom about where to put source files, where to put test files, where to put compiled files, and so on. Maven takes away that freedom. With this freedom, all the confusion about locations also goes. In Maven, there is a specific directory structure for everything. The following table shows a few of the most common locations:

`/src/main/scala`	Source code in Scala
`/src/main/java`	Source code in Java
`/src/main/resources`	Resources to be used by source code such as configuration files
`/src/test/scala`	Test code in Scala
`/src/test/java`	Test code in Java
`/src/test/resources`	Resources to be used by test code such as configuration files

- **Declarative dependency management**: In Maven, every library is defined by following three coordinates:

`groupId`	A logical way of grouping libraries similar to a package in Java/Scala, which has to be at least the domain name you own—for example, `org.apache.spark`
`artifactId`	The name of the project and JAR
`version`	Standard version numbers

In `pom.xml` (the configuration file that tells Maven all the information about a project), dependencies are declared in the form of these three coordinates. There is no need to search over the Internet and download, unpack, and copy libraries. All you need to do is to provide three coordinates of the dependency JAR you need and Maven will do the rest for you. The following is an example of using a JUnit dependency:

```
<dependency>
  <groupId>junit</groupId>
  <artifactId>junit</artifactId>
  <version>4.12</version>
</dependency>
```

This makes dependency management including transitive dependencies very easy. Build tools that came after Maven such as SBT and Gradle also follow these two rules as-is and provide enhancements in other aspects.

Getting ready

From this recipe onwards, this chapter assumes you have installed Eclipse. Please visit `http://www.eclipse.org` for details.

How to do it...

Let's see how to install the Maven plugin for Eclipse:

1. Open Eclipse and navigate to **Help** | **Install New Software**.
2. Click on the **Work with** drop-down menu.
3. Select the <eclipse version> update site.
4. Click on **Collaboration tools**.

5. Check Maven's integration with Eclipse, as in the following screenshot:

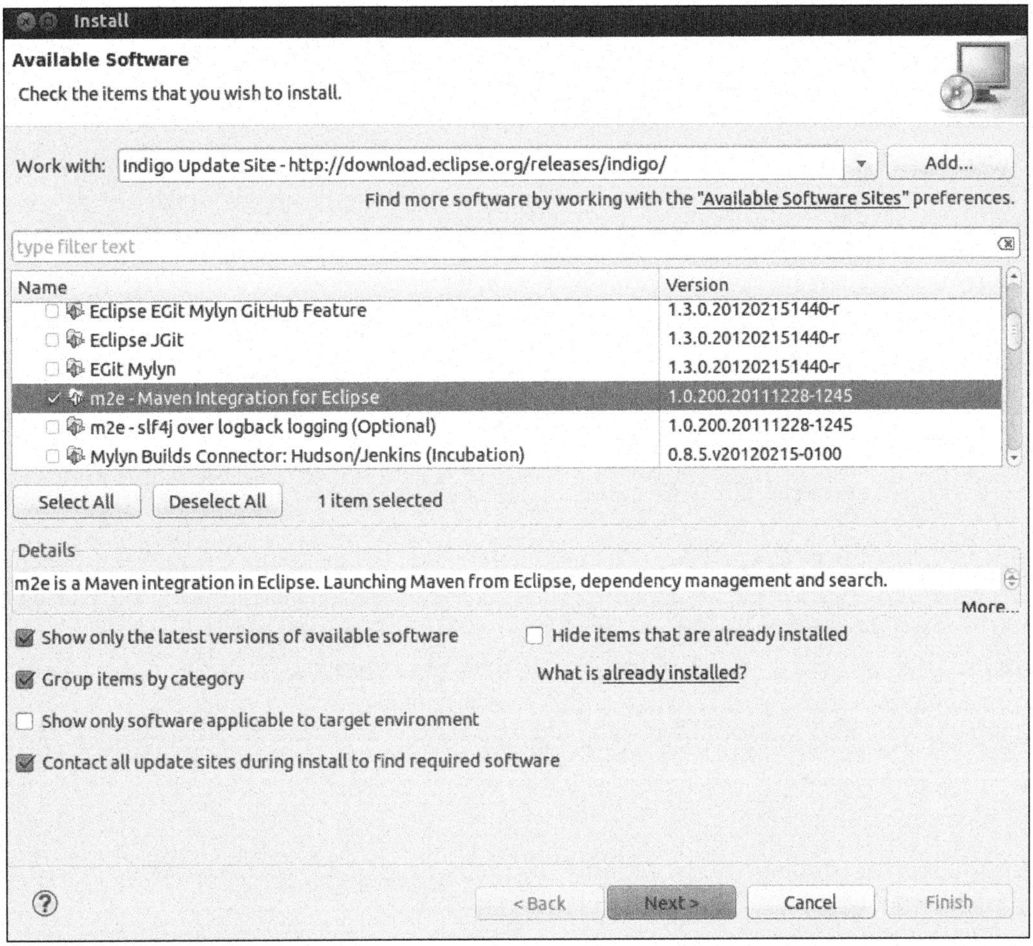

6. Click on **Next** and then click on **Finish**.

   There will be a prompt to restart Eclipse and Maven will be installed after the restart.

Now let's see how we can install the Scala plugin for Eclipse:

1. Open Eclipse and navigate to **Help** | **Install New Software**.
2. Click on the **Work with** drop-down menu.
3. Select the <eclipse version> update site.
4. Type `http://download.scala-ide.org/sdk/helium/e38/scala210/stable/site`.
5. Press *Enter*.

6. Select **Scala IDE for Eclipse**:

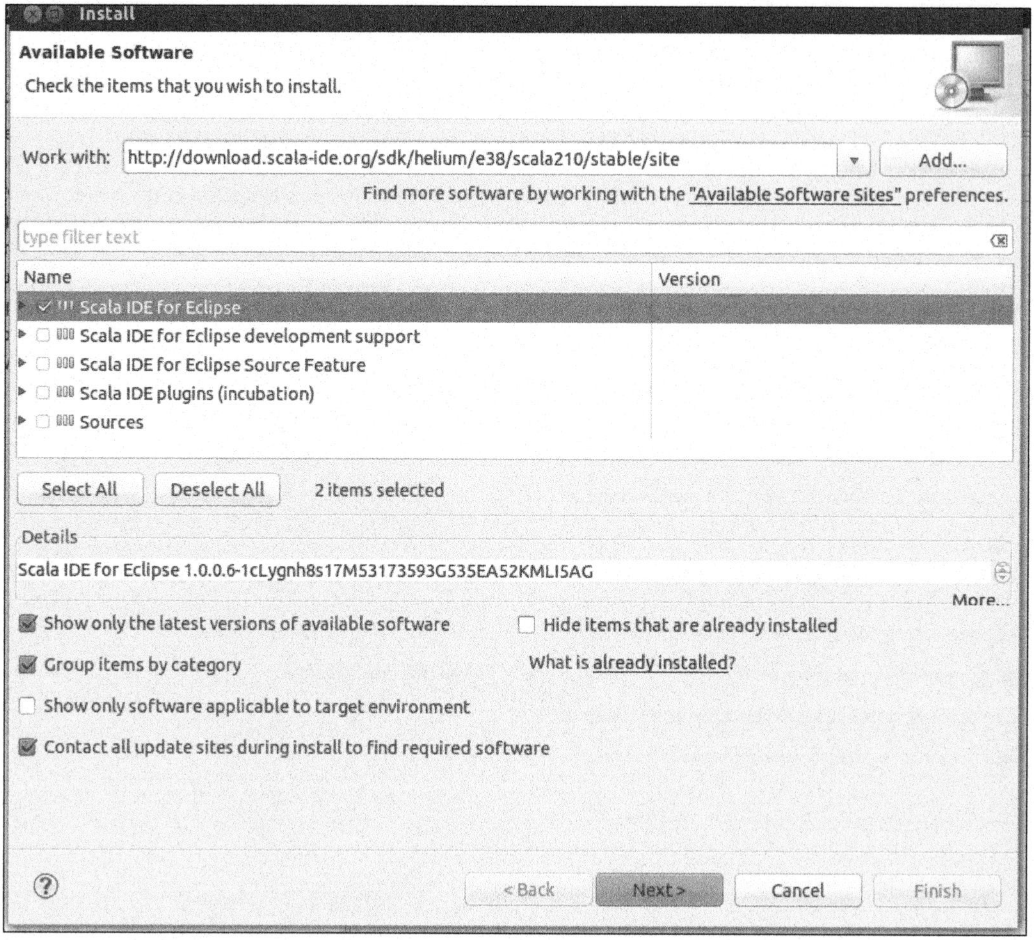

7. Click on **Next** and then click on **Finish**. You will be prompted to restart Eclipse and Scala will be installed after the restart.
8. Navigate to **Window** | **Open Perspective** | **Scala**.

Eclipse is now ready for Scala development!

Developing Spark applications in Eclipse with SBT

Simple Build Tool (**SBT**) is a build tool made especially for Scala-based development. SBT follows Maven-based naming conventions and declarative dependency management.

SBT provides the following enhancements over Maven:

- Dependencies are in the form of key-value pairs in the `build.sbt` file as opposed to `pom.xml` in Maven
- It provides a shell that makes it very handy to perform build operations
- For simple projects without dependencies, you do not even need the `build.sbt` file

In `build.sbt`, the first line is the project definition:

```
lazy val root = (project in file("."))
```

Each project has an immutable map of key-value pairs. This map is changed by settings in SBT like so:

```
lazy val root = (project in file("."))
  settings(
    name := "wordcount"
  )
```

Every change in the settings leads to a new map, as it's an immutable map.

How to do it...

Here's how we go about adding the `sbteclipse` plugin:

1. Add this to the global plugin file:

   ```
   $ mkdir /home/hduser/.sbt/0.13/plugins
   ```

   ```
   $ echo addSbtPlugin("com.typesafe.sbteclipse" % "sbteclipse-plugin" % "2.5.0" )  > /home/hduser/.sbt/0.12/plugins/plugin.sbt
   ```

   Alternatively, you can add the following to your project:

   ```
   $ cd <project-home>
   ```

   ```
   $ echo addSbtPlugin("com.typesafe.sbteclipse" % "sbteclipse-plugin" % "2.5.0" )  > plugin.sbt
   ```

2. Start the `sbt` shell without any arguments:

   ```
   $sbt
   ```

3. Type `eclipse` and it will make an Eclipse-ready project:

   ```
   $ eclipse
   ```

4. Now you can navigate to **File** | **Import** | **Import existing project into workspace** to load the project into Eclipse.

Now you can develop the Spark application in Scala using Eclipse and SBT.

Developing a Spark application in IntelliJ IDEA with Maven

IntelliJ IDEA comes bundled with support for Maven. We will see how to create a new Maven project in this recipe.

How to do it...

Perform the following steps to develop a Spark application on IntelliJ IDEA with Maven:

1. Select **Maven** in new project window and click on **Next**:

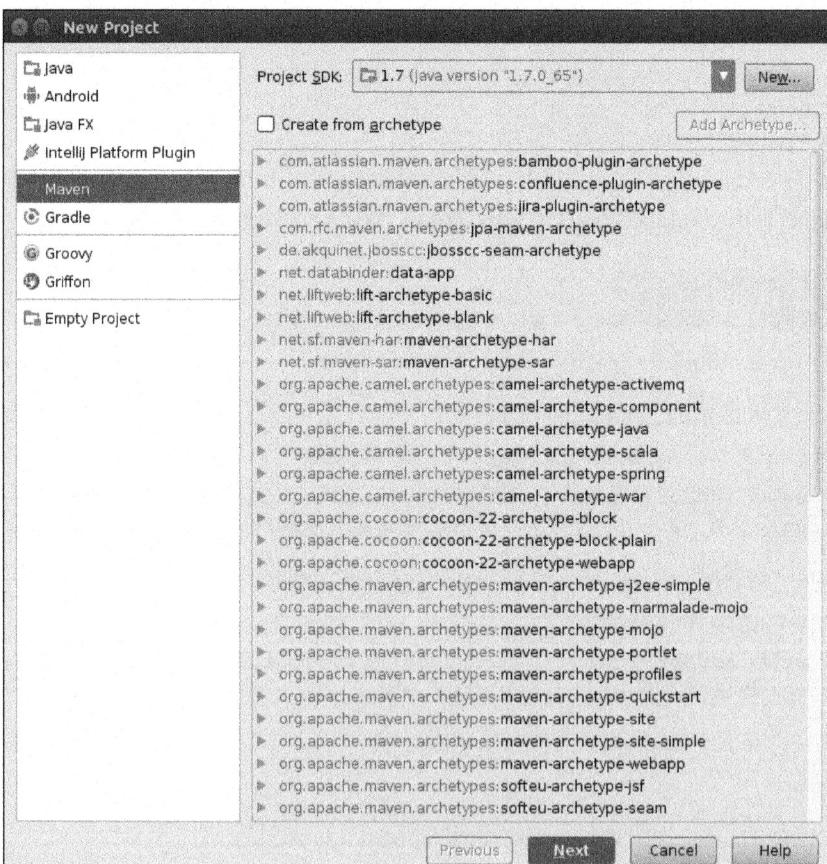

2. Enter three dimensions of the project:

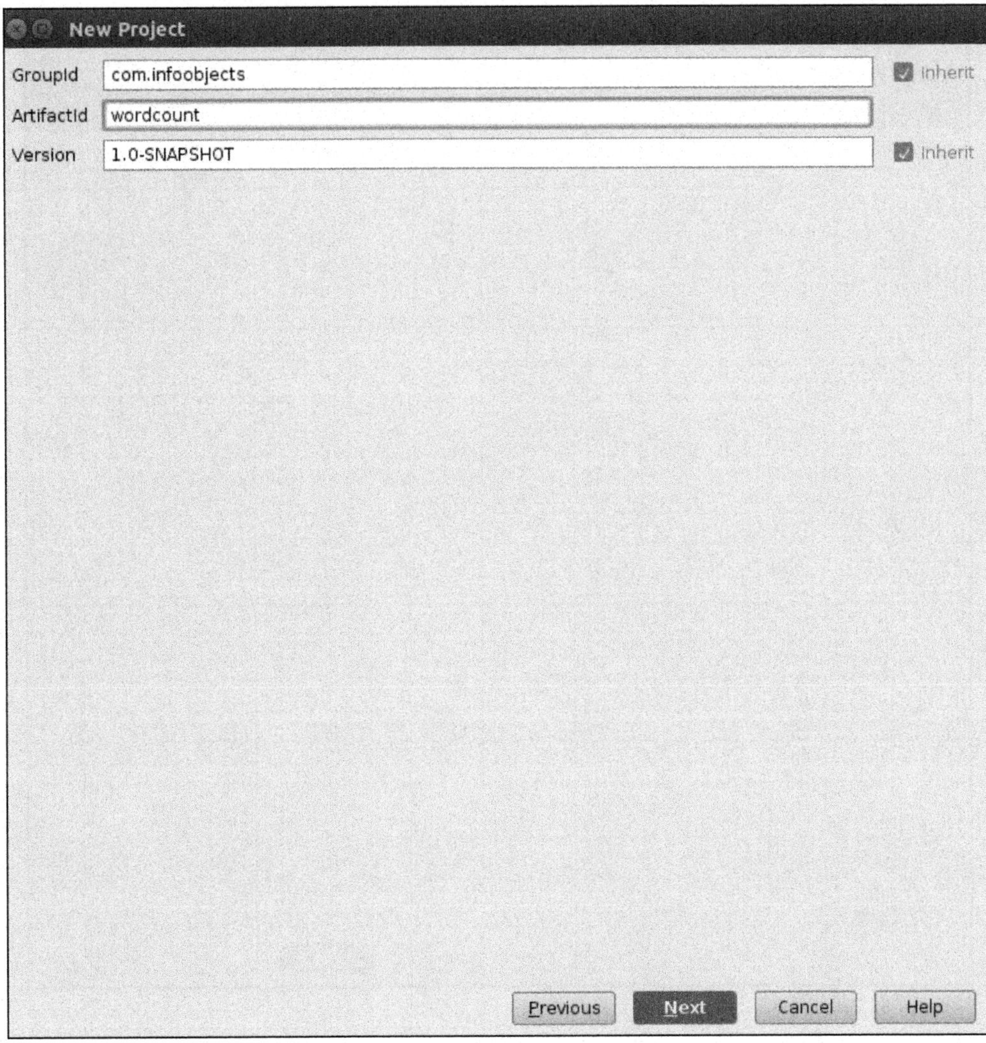

3. Enter the project's name and location:

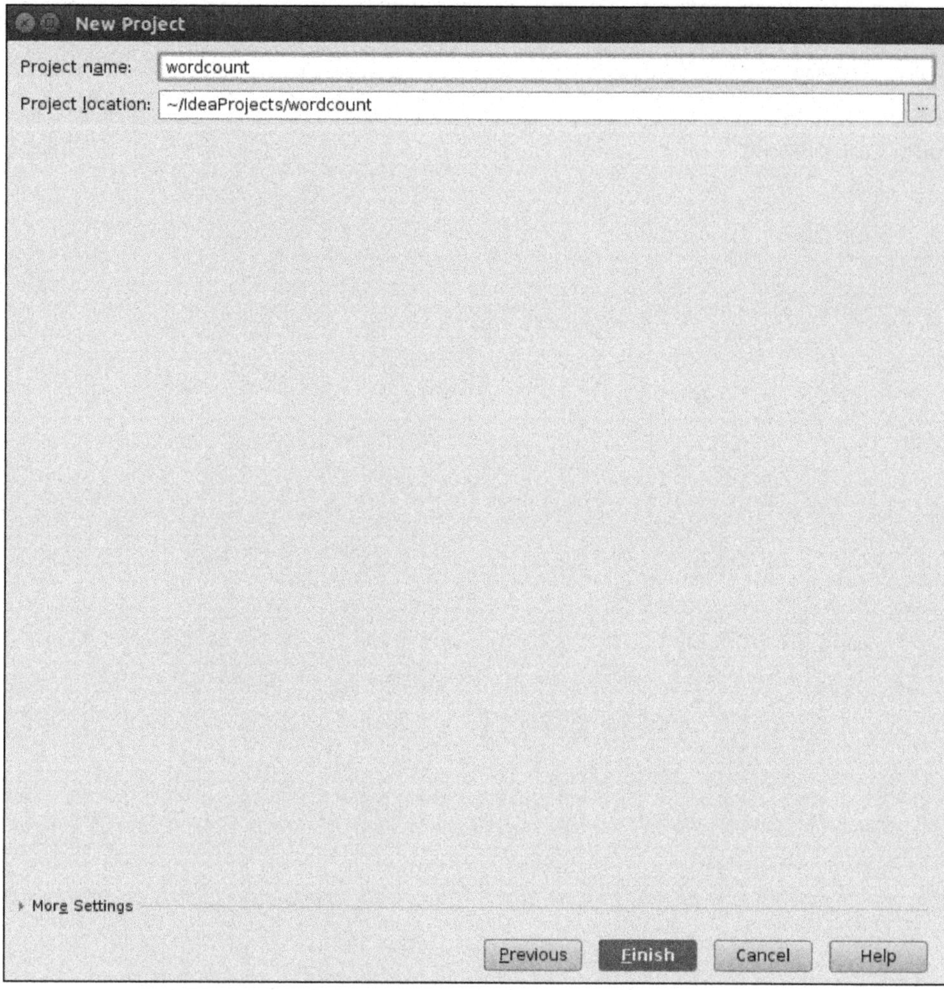

4. Click on **Finish** and the Maven project is ready.

Developing a Spark application in IntelliJ IDEA with SBT

Before Eclipse became famous, IntelliJ IDEA was considered best of the breed in IDEs. IDEA has not shed its former glory yet and a lot of developers love IDEA. IDEA also has a community edition, which is free. IDEA provides native support for SBT, which makes it ideal for SBT and Scala development.

How to do it...

Perform the following steps to develop a Spark application on IntelliJ IDEA with SBT:

1. Add the `sbt-idea` plugin.
2. Add to the global plugin file:

   ```
   $mkdir /home/hduser/.sbt/0.13/plugins
   $echo addSbtPlugin("com.github.mpeltone" % "sbt-idea" % "1.6.0" )
   > /home/hduser/.sbt/0.12/plugins/plugin.sbt
   ```

   Alternatively, you can add to your project as well:

   ```
   $cd <project-home>
   $ echo addSbtPlugin("com.github.mpeltone" % "sbt-idea" % "1.6.0" )
   > plugin.sbt
   ```

IDEA is ready to use with SBT.

Now you can develop Spark code using Scala and build using SBT.

3

External Data Sources

One of the strengths of Spark is that it provides a single runtime that can connect with various underlying data sources.

In this chapter, we will connect to different data sources. This chapter is divided into the following recipes:

- Loading data from the local filesystem
- Loading data from HDFS
- Loading data from HDFS using a custom InputFormat
- Loading data from Amazon S3
- Loading data from Apache Cassandra
- Loading data from relational databases

Introduction

Spark provides a unified runtime for big data. HDFS, which is Hadoop's filesystem, is the most used storage platform for Spark as it provides cost-effective storage for unstructured and semi-structured data on commodity hardware. Spark is not limited to HDFS and can work with any Hadoop-supported storage.

Hadoop supported storage means a storage format that can work with Hadoop's `InputFormat` and `OutputFormat` interfaces. `InputFormat` is responsible for creating `InputSplits` from input data and dividing it further into records. `OutputFormat` is responsible for writing to storage.

We will start with writing to the local filesystem and then move over to loading data from HDFS. In the *Loading data from HDFS* recipe, we will cover the most common file format: regular text files. In the next recipe, we will cover how to use any `InputFormat` interface to load data in Spark. We will also explore loading data stored in Amazon S3, a leading cloud storage platform.

We will explore loading data from Apache Cassandra, which is a NoSQL database. Finally, we will explore loading data from a relational database.

Loading data from the local filesystem

Though the local filesystem is not a good fit to store big data due to disk size limitations and lack of distributed nature, technically you can load data in distributed systems using the local filesystem. But then the file/directory you are accessing has to be available on each node.

Please note that if you are planning to use this feature to load side data, it is not a good idea. To load side data, Spark has a broadcast variable feature, which will be discussed in upcoming chapters.

In this recipe, we will look at how to load data in Spark from the local filesystem.

How to do it...

Let's start with the example of Shakespeare's "to be or not to be":

1. Create the `words` directory by using the following command:
   ```
   $ mkdir words
   ```
2. Get into the `words` directory:
   ```
   $ cd words
   ```
3. Create the `sh.txt` text file and enter `"to be or not to be"` in it:
   ```
   $ echo "to be or not to be" > sh.txt
   ```
4. Start the Spark shell:
   ```
   $ spark-shell
   ```
5. Load the `words` directory as RDD:
   ```
   scala> val words = sc.textFile("file:///home/hduser/words")
   ```
6. Count the number of lines:
   ```
   scala> words.count
   ```
7. Divide the line (or lines) into multiple words:
   ```
   scala> val wordsFlatMap = words.flatMap(_.split("\\W+"))
   ```
8. Convert `word` to (word,1)—that is, output `1` as the value for each occurrence of `word` as a key:
   ```
   scala> val wordsMap = wordsFlatMap.map( w => (w,1))
   ```

9. Use the `reduceByKey` method to add the number of occurrences for each word as a key (this function works on two consecutive values at a time, represented by `a` and `b`):

```
scala> val wordCount = wordsMap.reduceByKey( (a,b) => (a+b))
```

10. Print the RDD:

```
scala> wordCount.collect.foreach(println)
```

11. Doing all of the preceding operations in one step is as follows:

```
scala> sc.textFile("file:///home/hduser/ words"). flatMap(_.
split("\\W+")).map( w => (w,1)). reduceByKey( (a,b) => (a+b)).
foreach(println)
```

This gives the following output:

```
(to,2)
(not,1)
(be,2)
(or,1)
```

Loading data from HDFS

HDFS is the most widely used big data storage system. One of the reasons for the wide adoption of HDFS is schema-on-read. What this means is that HDFS does not put any restriction on data when data is being written. Any and all kinds of data are welcome and can be stored in a raw format. This feature makes it ideal storage for raw unstructured data and semi-structured data.

When it comes to reading data, even unstructured data needs to be given some structure to make sense. Hadoop uses `InputFormat` to determine how to read the data. Spark provides complete support for Hadoop's `InputFormat` so anything that can be read by Hadoop can be read by Spark as well.

The default `InputFormat` is `TextInputFormat`. `TextInputFormat` takes the byte offset of a line as a key and the content of a line as a value. Spark uses the `sc.textFile` method to read using `TextInputFormat`. It ignores the byte offset and creates an RDD of strings.

Sometimes the filename itself contains useful information, for example, time-series data. In that case, you may want to read each file separately. The `sc.wholeTextFiles` method allows you to do that. It creates an RDD with the filename and path (for example, `hdfs://localhost:9000/user/hduser/words`) as a key and the content of the whole file as the value.

Spark also supports reading various serialization and compression-friendly formats such as Avro, Parquet, and JSON using DataFrames. These formats will be covered in coming chapters.

In this recipe, we will look at how to load data in the Spark shell from HDFS.

How to do it...

Let's do the word count, which counts the number of occurrences of each word. In this recipe, we will load data from HDFS:

1. Create the `words` directory by using the following command:

   ```
   $ mkdir words
   ```

2. Change the directory to `words`:

   ```
   $ cd words
   ```

3. Create the `sh.txt text` file and enter `"to be or not to be"` in it:

   ```
   $ echo "to be or not to be" > sh.txt
   ```

4. Start the Spark shell:

   ```
   $ spark-shell
   ```

5. Load the `words` directory as the RDD:

   ```
   scala> val words = sc.textFile("hdfs://localhost:9000/user/hduser/
   words")
   ```

> The `sc.textFile` method also supports passing an additional argument for the number of partitions. By default, Spark creates one partition for each `InputSplit` class, which roughly corresponds to one block.
>
> You can ask for a higher number of partitions. It works really well for compute-intensive jobs such as in machine learning. As one partition cannot contain more than one block, having fewer partitions than blocks is not allowed.

6. Count the number of lines (the result will be `1`):

   ```
   scala> words.count
   ```

7. Divide the line (or lines) into multiple words:

   ```
   scala> val wordsFlatMap = words.flatMap(_.split("\\W+"))
   ```

8. Convert word to (word,1)—that is, output `1` as a value for each occurrence of `word` as a key:

   ```
   scala> val wordsMap = wordsFlatMap.map( w => (w,1))
   ```

9. Use the `reduceByKey` method to add the number of occurrences of each word as a key (this function works on two consecutive values at a time, represented by `a` and `b`):

   ```
   scala> val wordCount = wordsMap.reduceByKey( (a,b) => (a+b))
   ```

10. Print the RDD:

```
scala> wordCount.collect.foreach(println)
```

11. Doing all of the preceding operations in one step is as follows:

```
scala> sc.textFile("hdfs://localhost:9000/user/hduser/words").
flatMap(_.split("\\W+")).map( w => (w,1)). reduceByKey( (a,b) =>
(a+b)).foreach(println)
```

This gives the following output:

There's more...

Sometimes we need to access the whole file at once. Sometimes the filename contains useful data like in the case of time-series. Sometimes you need to process more than one line as a record. `sparkContext.wholeTextFiles` comes to the rescue here. We will look at weather dataset from `ftp://ftp.ncdc.noaa.gov/pub/data/noaa/`.

Here's what a top-level directory looks like:

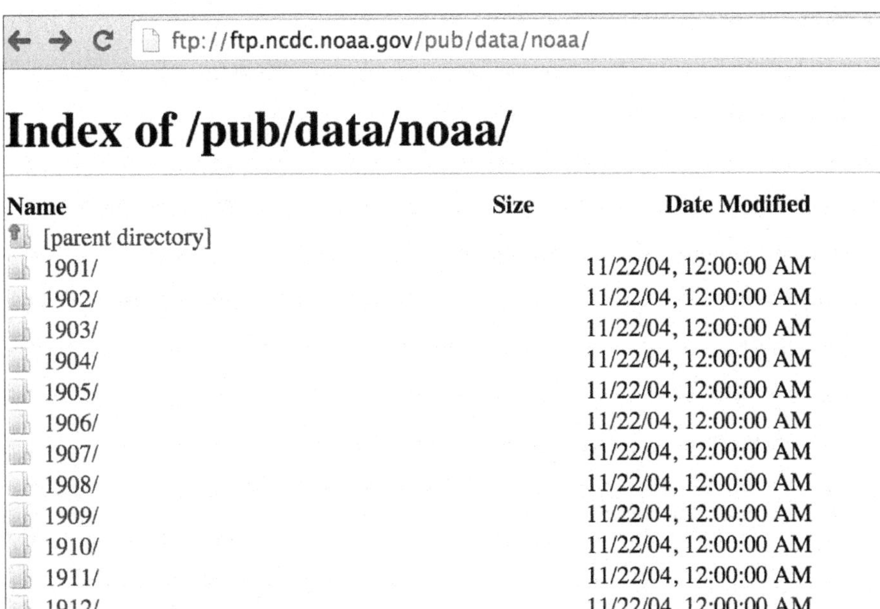
ftp://ftp.ncdc.noaa.gov/pub/data/noaa/

Index of /pub/data/noaa/

Name	Size	Date Modified
[parent directory]		
1901/		11/22/04, 12:00:00 AM
1902/		11/22/04, 12:00:00 AM
1903/		11/22/04, 12:00:00 AM
1904/		11/22/04, 12:00:00 AM
1905/		11/22/04, 12:00:00 AM
1906/		11/22/04, 12:00:00 AM
1907/		11/22/04, 12:00:00 AM
1908/		11/22/04, 12:00:00 AM
1909/		11/22/04, 12:00:00 AM
1910/		11/22/04, 12:00:00 AM
1911/		11/22/04, 12:00:00 AM
1912/		11/22/04, 12:00:00 AM

Looking into a particular year directory—for example, 1901 resembles the following screenshot:

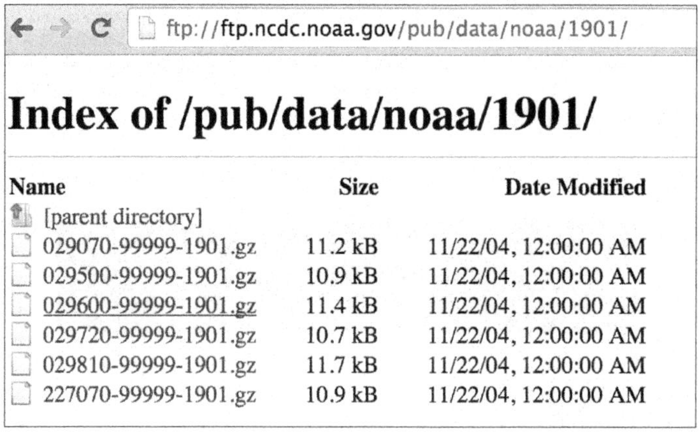

Data here is divided in such a way that each filename contains useful information, that is, USAF-WBAN-year, where USAF is the US air force station number and WBAN is the weather bureau army navy location number.

You will also notice that all files are compressed as gzip with a `.gz` extension. Compression is handled automatically so all you need to do is to upload data in HDFS. We will come back to this dataset in the coming chapters.

Since the whole dataset is not large, it can be uploaded in HDFS in the pseudo-distributed mode also:

1. Download data:

   ```
   $ wget -r ftp://ftp.ncdc.noaa.gov/pub/data/noaa/
   ```

2. Load the weather data in HDFS:

   ```
   $ hdfs dfs -put ftp.ncdc.noaa.gov/pub/data/noaa weather/
   ```

3. Start the Spark shell:

   ```
   $ spark-shell
   ```

4. Load weather data for 1901 in the RDD:

   ```
   scala> val weatherFileRDD = sc.wholeTextFiles("hdfs://
   localhost:9000/user/hduser/weather/1901")
   ```

5. Cache weather in the RDD so that it is not recomputed every time it's accessed:

   ```
   scala> val weatherRDD = weatherFileRDD.cache
   ```

> In Spark, there are various StorageLevels at which the RDD can be persisted. `rdd.cache` is a shorthand for the `rdd.persist(MEMORY_ONLY)` StorageLevel.

6. Count the number of elements:

```
scala> weatherRDD.count
```

7. Since the whole contents of a file are loaded as an element, we need to manually interpret the data, so let's load the first element:

```
scala> val firstElement = weatherRDD.first
```

8. Read the value of the first RDD:

```
scala> val firstValue = firstElement._2
```

   The `firstElement` contains tuples in the form (string, string). Tuples can be accessed in two ways:

   - Using a positional function starting with `_1`.
   - Using the `productElement` method, for example, `tuple.productElement(0)`. Indexes here start with `0` like most other methods.

9. Split `firstValue` by lines:

```
scala> val firstVals = firstValue.split("\\n")
```

10. Count the number of elements in `firstVals`:

```
scala> firstVals.size
```

11. The schema of weather data is very rich with the position of the text working as a delimiter. You can get more information about schemas at the national weather service website. Let's get wind speed, which is from section 66-69 (in meter/sec):

```
scala> val windSpeed = firstVals.map(line => line.substring(65,69)
```

Loading data from HDFS using a custom InputFormat

Sometimes you need to load data in a specific format and `TextInputFormat` is not a good fit for that. Spark provides two methods for this purpose:

- `sparkContext.hadoopFile`: This supports the old MapReduce API
- `sparkContext.newAPIHadoopFile`: This supports the new MapReduce API

These two methods provide support for all of Hadoop's built-in InputFormats interfaces as well as any custom `InputFormat`.

How to do it...

We are going to load text data in key-value format and load it in Spark using `KeyValueTextInputFormat`:

1. Create the `currency` directory by using the following command:

   ```
   $ mkdir currency
   ```

2. Change the current directory to `currency`:

   ```
   $ cd currency
   ```

3. Create the `na.txt` text file and enter currency values in key-value format delimited by tab (key: country, value: currency):

   ```
   $ vi na.txt
   United States of America        US Dollar
   Canada  Canadian Dollar
   Mexico  Peso
   ```

   You can create more files for each continent.

4. Upload the `currency` folder to HDFS:

   ```
   $ hdfs dfs -put currency /user/hduser/currency
   ```

5. Start the Spark shell:

   ```
   $ spark-shell
   ```

6. Import statements:

   ```
   scala> import org.apache.hadoop.io.Text
   scala> import org.apache.hadoop.mapreduce.lib.input.
   KeyValueTextInputFormat
   ```

7. Load the `currency` directory as the RDD:

   ```
   val currencyFile = sc.newAPIHadoopFile("hdfs://localhost:9000/
   user/hduser/currency",classOf[KeyValueTextInputFormat],classOf[Tex
   t],classOf[Text])
   ```

8. Convert it from tuple of (Text,Text) to tuple of (String,String):

   ```
   val currencyRDD = currencyFile.map( t => (t._1.toString,t._2.
   toString))
   ```

9. Count the number of elements in the RDD:

   ```
   scala> currencyRDD.count
   ```

10. Print the values:

    ```
    scala> currencyRDD.collect.foreach(println)
    ```

    ```
    (United States of America,US Dollar)
    (Canada,Canadian Dollar)
    (Mexico,Peso)
    ```

[You can use this approach to load data in any Hadoop-supported `InputFormat` interface.]

Loading data from Amazon S3

Amazon **Simple Storage Service** (**S3**) provides developers and IT teams with a secure, durable, and scalable storage platform. The biggest advantage of Amazon S3 is that there is no up-front IT investment and companies can build capacity (just by clicking a button a button) as they need.

Though Amazon S3 can be used with any compute platform, it integrates really well with Amazon's cloud services such as Amazon **Elastic Compute Cloud** (**EC2**) and Amazon **Elastic Block Storage** (**EBS**). For this reason, companies who use **Amazon Web Services** (**AWS**) are likely to have significant data is already stored on Amazon S3.

This makes a good case for loading data in Spark from Amazon S3 and that is exactly what this recipe is about.

How to do it...

Let's start with the AWS portal:

1. Go to `http://aws.amazon.com` and log in with your username and password.
2. Once logged in, navigate to **Storage & Content Delivery** | **S3** | **Create Bucket**:

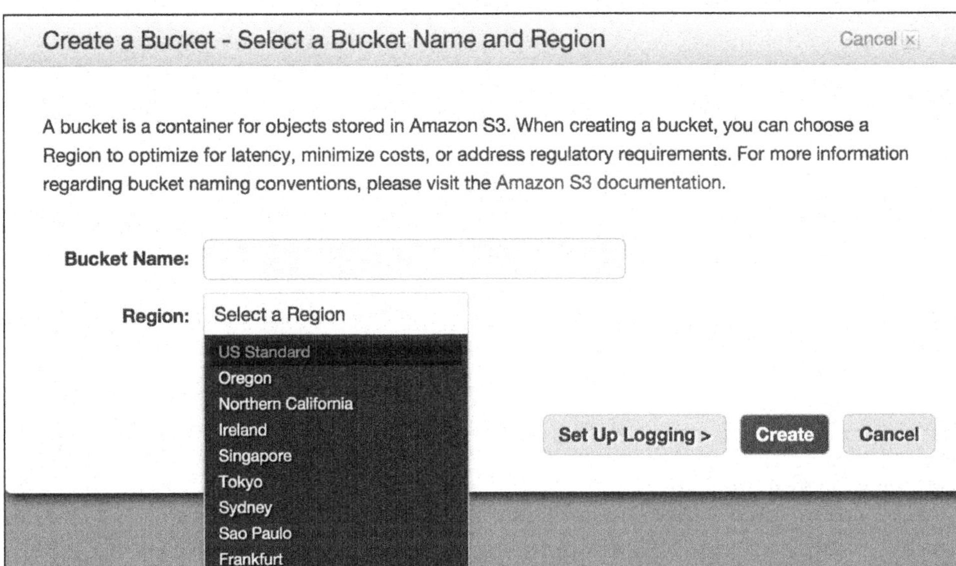

3. Enter the bucket name—for example, `com.infoobjects.wordcount`. Please make sure you enter a unique bucket name (no two S3 buckets can have the same name globally).
4. Select **Region**, click on **Create**, and then on the bucket name you created and you will see the following screen:

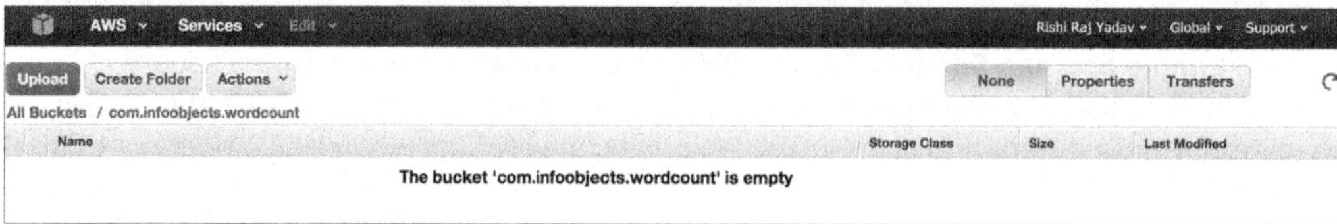

5. Click on **Create Folder** and enter `words` as the folder name.
6. Create the `sh.txt` text file on the local filesystem:

```
$ echo "to be or not to be" > sh.txt
```

7. Navigate to **Words** | **Upload** | **Add Files** and choose `sh.txt` from the dialog box, as shown in the following screenshot:

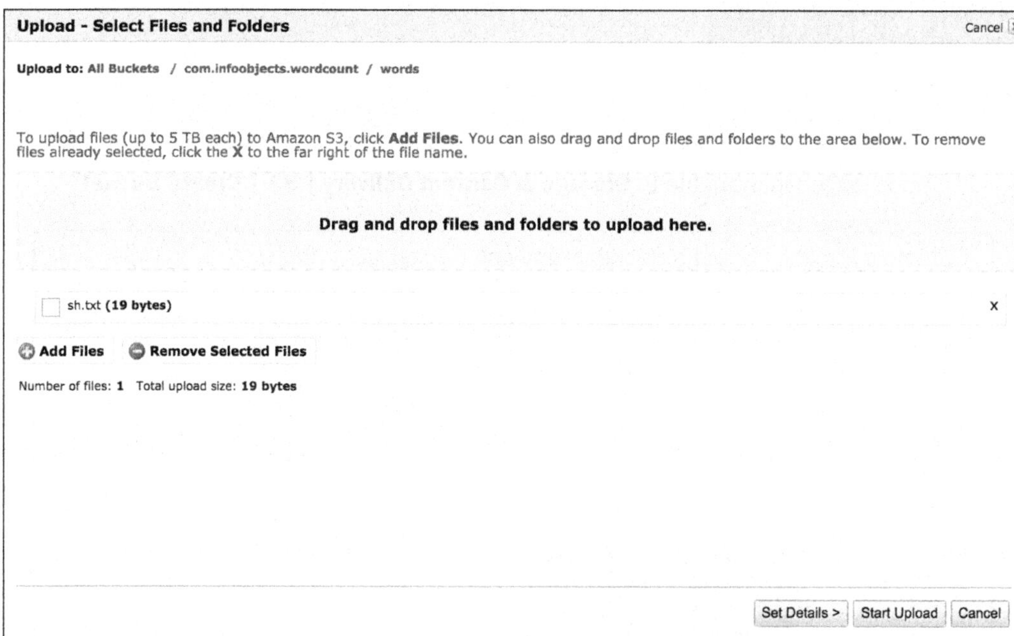

8. Click on **Start Upload**.

9. Select **sh.txt** and click on **Properties** and it will show you details of the file:

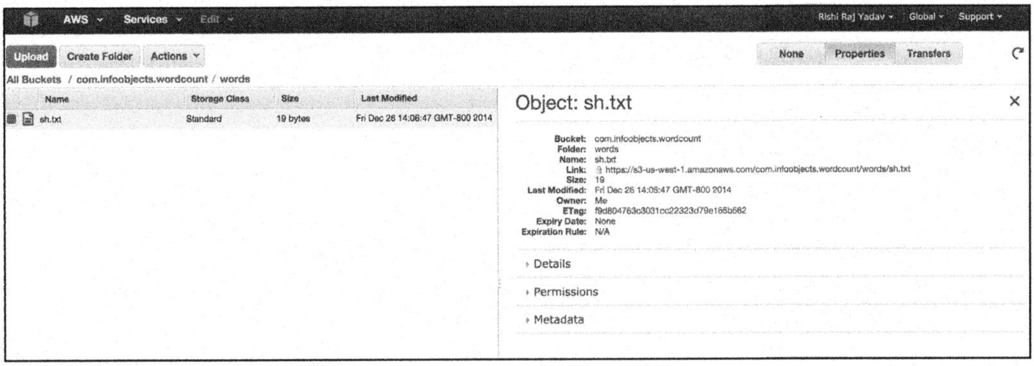

10. Set `AWS_ACCESS_KEY` and `AWS_SECRET_ACCESS_KEY` as environment variables.
11. Open the Spark shell and load the `words` directory from `s3` in the `words` RDD:

```
scala>  val words = sc.textFile("s3n://com.infoobjects.wordcount/
words")
```

Now the RDD is loaded and you can continue doing regular transformations and actions on the RDD.

> Sometimes there is confusion between `s3://` and `s3n://`. `s3n://` means a regular file sitting in the S3 bucket but readable and writable by the outside world. This filesystem puts a 5 GB limit on the file size.
>
> `s3://` means an HDFS file sitting in the S3 bucket. It is a block-based filesystem. The filesystem requires you to dedicate a bucket for this filesystem. There is no limit on file size in this system.

Loading data from Apache Cassandra

Apache Cassandra is a NoSQL database with a masterless ring cluster structure. While HDFS is a good fit for streaming data access, it does not work well with random access. For example, HDFS will work well when your average file size is 100 MB and you want to read the whole file. If you frequently access the *n*th line in a file or some other part as a record, HDFS would be too slow.

Relational databases have traditionally provided a solution to that, providing low latency, random access, but they do not work well with big data. NoSQL databases such as Cassandra fill the gap by providing relational database type access but in a distributed architecture on commodity servers.

In this recipe, we will load data from Cassandra as a Spark RDD. To make that happen Datastax, the company behind Cassandra, has contributed `spark-cassandra-connector`. This connector lets you load Cassandra tables as Spark RDDs, write Spark RDDs back to Cassandra, and execute CQL queries.

How to do it...

Perform the following steps to load data from Cassandra:

1. Create a keyspace named `people` in Cassandra using the CQL shell:

   ```
   cqlsh> CREATE KEYSPACE people WITH replication = {'class':
   'SimpleStrategy', 'replication_factor': 1 };
   ```

2. Create a column family (from CQL 3.0 onwards, it can also be called a **table**) `person` in newer versions of Cassandra:

   ```
   cqlsh> create columnfamily person(id int primary key,first_name
   varchar,last_name varchar);
   ```

3. Insert a few records in the column family:

   ```
   cqlsh> insert into person(id,first_name,last_name)
   values(1,'Barack','Obama');
   cqlsh> insert into person(id,first_name,last_name)
   values(2,'Joe','Smith');
   ```

4. Add Cassandra connector dependency to SBT:

   ```
   "com.datastax.spark" %% "spark-cassandra-connector" % 1.2.0
   ```

5. You can also add the Cassandra dependency to Maven:

   ```
   <dependency>
     <groupId>com.datastax.spark</groupId>
     <artifactId>spark-cassandra-connector_2.10</artifactId>
     <version>1.2.0</version>
   </dependency>
   ```

   Alternatively, you can also download the `spark-cassandra-connector` JAR to use directly with the Spark shell:

   ```
   $ wget http://central.maven.org/maven2/com/datastax/spark/spark-
   cassandra-connector_2.10/1.1.0/spark-cassandra-connector_2.10-
   1.2.0.jar
   ```

   > If you would like to build the `uber` JAR with all dependencies, refer to the *There's more...* section.

6. Now start the Spark shell.
7. Set the `spark.cassandra.connection.host` property in the Spark shell:

```
scala> sc.getConf.set("spark.cassandra.connection.host",
"localhost")
```

8. Import Cassandra-specific libraries:

```
scala> import com.datastax.spark.connector._
```

9. Load the `person` column family as an RDD:

```
scala> val personRDD = sc.cassandraTable("people","person")
```

10. Count the number of records in the RDD:

```
scala> personRDD.count
```

11. Print data in the RDD:

```
scala> personRDD.collect.foreach(println)
```

12. Retrieve the first row:

```
scala> val firstRow = personRDD.first
```

13. Get the column names:

```
scala> firstRow.columnNames
```

14. Cassandra can also be accessed through Spark SQL. It has a wrapper around `SQLContext` called `CassandraSQLContext`; let's load it:

```
scala> val cc = new org.apache.spark.sql.cassandra.
CassandraSQLContext(sc)
```

15. Load the `person` data as `SchemaRDD`:

```
scala> val p = cc.sql("select * from people.person")
```

16. Retrieve the `person` data:

```
scala> p.collect.foreach(println)
```

There's more...

Spark Cassandra's connector library has a lot of dependencies. The connector itself and several of its dependencies are third-party to Spark and are not available as part of the Spark installation.

These dependencies need to be made available to the driver as well as executors at runtime. One way to do this is to bundle all transitive dependencies, but that is a laborious and error-prone process. The recommended approach is to bundle all the dependencies along with the connector library. This will result in a fat JAR, popularly known as the `uber` JAR.

SBT provides the `sbt-assembly` plugin, which makes creating `uber` JARs very easy. The following are the steps to create an `uber` JAR for `spark-cassandra-connector`. These steps are general enough so that you can use them to create any `uber` JAR:

1. Create a folder named `uber`:

   ```
   $ mkdir uber
   ```

2. Change the directory to `uber`:

   ```
   $ cd uber
   ```

3. Open the SBT prompt:

   ```
   $ sbt
   ```

4. Give this project a name `sc-uber`:

   ```
   > set name := "sc-uber"
   ```

5. Save the session:

   ```
   > session save
   ```

6. Exit the session:

   ```
   > exit
   ```

   This will create `build.sbt`, `project`, and `target` folders in the `uber` folder as shown in the following screenshot:

   ```
   hduser@localhost:~/uber$ ls
   build.sbt  project  target
   ```

7. Add the `spark-cassandra-driver` dependency to `build.sbt` at the end after leaving a blank line as shown in the following screenshot:

   ```
   $ vi buid.sbt
   ```

```
name := "sc-uber"

libraryDependencies += "com.datastax.spark" %% "spark-cassandra-connector" % "1.1.0"
```

8. We will use `MergeStrategy.first` as the default. Besides that, there are some files, such as `manifest.mf`, that every JAR bundles for metadata, and we can simply discard them. We are going to use `MergeStrategy.discard` for that. The following is the screenshot of `build.sbt` with `assemblyMergeStrategy` added:

```
name := "sc-uber"

libraryDependencies += "com.datastax.spark" %% "spark-cassandra-connector" % "1.1.0"

assemblyMergeStrategy in assembly := {
 case PathList("META-INF", xs @ _*) =>
    (xs map {_.toLowerCase}) match {
      case ("manifest.mf" :: Nil) | ("index.list" :: Nil) | ("dependencies" :: Nil) => MergeStrategy.discard
      case _ => MergeStrategy.discard
    }
 case _  => MergeStrategy.first
}
```

9. Now create `plugins.sbt` in the `project` folder and type the following for the `sbt-assembly` plugin:

   ```
   addSbtPlugin("com.eed3si9n" % "sbt-assembly" % "0.12.0")
   ```

10. We are ready to build (`assembly`) a JAR now:

   ```
   $ sbt assembly
   ```

   The `uber` JAR is now created in `target/scala-2.10/sc-uber-assembly-0.1-SNAPSHOT.jar`.

11. Copy it to a suitable location where you keep all third-party JARs—for example, `/home/hduser/thirdparty`—and rename it to an easier name (unless you like longer names):

   ```
   $ mv thirdparty/sc-uber-assembly-0.1-SNAPSHOT.jar  thirdparty/sc-uber.jar
   ```

12. Load the Spark shell with the `uber` JAR using `--jars`:

   ```
   $ spark-shell --jars thirdparty/sc-uber.jar
   ```

13. To submit the Scala code to a cluster, you can call `spark-submit` with the same JARS option:

   ```
   $ spark-submit --jars thirdparty/sc-uber.jar
   ```

Merge strategies in sbt-assembly

If multiple JARs have files with the same name and the same relative path, the default merge strategy for the `sbt-assembly` plugin is to verify that content is same for all the files and error out otherwise. This strategy is called `MergeStrategy.deduplicate`.

The following are the available merge strategies in the `sbt-assembly plugin`:

Strategy name	Description
`MergeStrategy.deduplicate`	The default strategy
`MergeStrategy.first`	Picks first file according to classpath
`MergeStrategy.last`	Picks last file according to classpath
`MergeStrategy.singleOrError`	Errors out (merge conflict not expected)
`MergeStrategy.concat`	Concatenates all matching files together
`MergeStrategy.filterDistinctLines`	Concatenates leaving out duplicates
`MergeStrategy.rename`	Renames files

Loading data from relational databases

A lot of important data lies in relational databases that Spark needs to query. JdbcRDD is a Spark feature that allows relational tables to be loaded as RDDs. This recipe will explain how to use JdbcRDD.

Spark SQL to be introduced in the next chapter includes a data source for JDBC. This should be preferred over the current recipe as results are returned as DataFrames (to be introduced in the next chapter), which can be easily processed by Spark SQL and also joined with other data sources.

Getting ready

Please make sure that the JDBC driver JAR is visible on the client node and all slaves nodes on which executor will run.

How to do it...

Perform the following steps to load data from relational databases:

1. Create a table named `person` in MySQL using the following DDL:

```
CREATE TABLE 'person' (
  'person_id' int(11) NOT NULL AUTO_INCREMENT,
  'first_name' varchar(30) DEFAULT NULL,
  'last_name' varchar(30) DEFAULT NULL,
  'gender' char(1) DEFAULT NULL,
  PRIMARY KEY ('person_id');
)
```

2. Insert some data:

```
Insert into person values('Barack','Obama','M');
Insert into person values('Bill','Clinton','M');
Insert into person values('Hillary','Clinton','F');
```

3. Download `mysql-connector-java-x.x.xx-bin.jar` from `http://dev.mysql.com/downloads/connector/j/`.

4. Make the MySQL driver available to the Spark shell and launch it:

```
$ spark-shell --jars /path-to-mysql-jar/mysql-connector-java-5.1.29-bin.jar
```

> Please note that `path-to-mysql-jar` is not the actual path name. You should use the actual path name.

5. Create variables for the username, password, and JDBC URL:

```
scala> val url="jdbc:mysql://localhost:3306/hadoopdb"
scala> val username = "hduser"
scala> val password = "******"
```

6. Import JdbcRDD:

```
scala> import org.apache.spark.rdd.JdbcRDD
```

7. Import JDBC-related classes:

```
scala> import java.sql.{Connection, DriverManager, ResultSet}
```

8. Create an instance of the JDBC driver:

```
scala> Class.forName("com.mysql.jdbc.Driver").newInstance
```

9. Load JdbcRDD:

```
scala> val myRDD = new JdbcRDD( sc, () =>
DriverManager.getConnection(url,username,password) ,
"select first_name,last_name,gender from person limit ?, ?",
1, 5, 2, r => r.getString("last_name") + ", " +
r.getString("first_name"))
```

10. Now query the results:

```
scala> myRDD.count
scala> myRDD.foreach(println)
```

11. Save the RDD to HDFS:

```
scala> myRDD.saveAsTextFile("hdfs://localhost:9000/user/hduser/person")
```

How it works...

JdbcRDD is an RDD that executes a SQL query on a JDBC connection and retrieves the results. The following is a JdbcRDD constructor:

```
JdbcRDD( SparkContext, getConnection: () => Connection,
sql: String, lowerBound: Long, upperBound: Long,
numPartitions: Int,  mapRow: (ResultSet) => T =
 JdbcRDD.resultSetToObjectArray)
```

The two ?'s are bind variables for a prepared statement inside JdbcRDD. The first ? is for the offset (lower bound), that is, which row should we start computing with, the second ? is for the limit (upper bound), that is, how many rows should we read.

JdbcRDD is a great way to load data in Spark directly from relational databases on an ad-hoc basis. If you would like to load data in bulk from RDBMS, there are other approaches that would work better, for example, Apache Sqoop is a powerful tool that imports and exports data from relational databases to HDFS.

4
Spark SQL

Spark SQL is a Spark module for processing a structured data. This chapter is divided into the following recipes:

- Understanding the Catalyst optimizer
- Creating HiveContext
- Inferring schema using case classes
- Programmatically specifying the schema
- Loading and saving data using the Parquet format
- Loading and saving data using the JSON format
- Loading and saving data from relational databases
- Loading and saving data from an arbitrary source

Introduction

Spark can process data from various data sources such as HDFS, Cassandra, HBase, and relational databases, including HDFS. Big data frameworks (unlike relational database systems) do not enforce schema while writing. HDFS is a perfect example where any arbitrary file is welcome during the write phase. Reading data is a different story, however. You need to give some structure to even completely unstructured data to make sense out of it. With this structured data, SQL comes very handy when it comes to analysis.

Spark SQL is a relatively new component in Spark ecosystem, introduced in Spark 1.0 for the first time. It incorporates a project named Shark, which was an attempt to make Hive run on Spark.

Hive is essentially a relational abstraction, which converts SQL queries to MapReduce jobs.

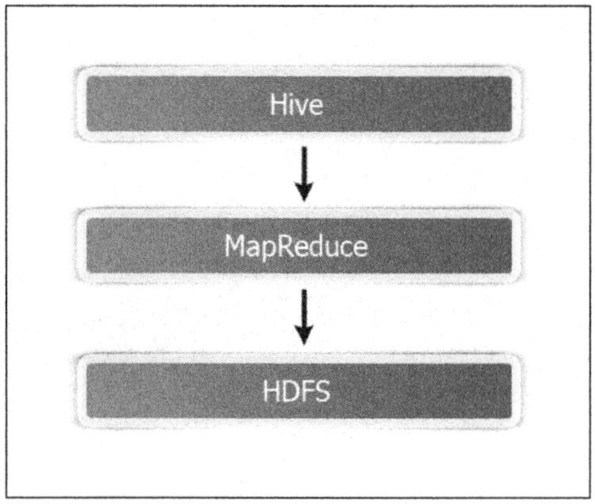

Shark replaced the MapReduce part with Spark while retaining most of the code base.

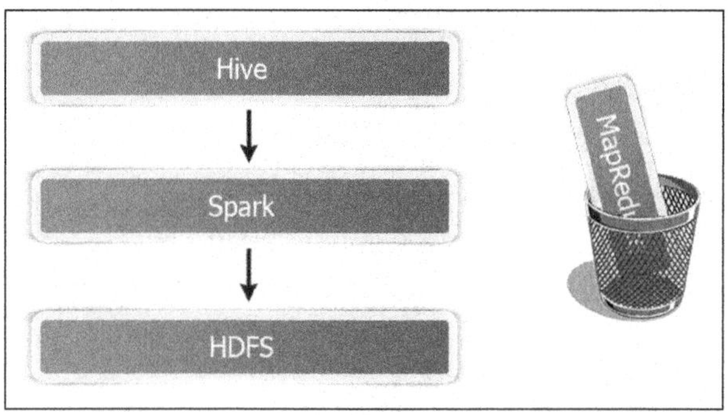

Initially, it worked fine, but very soon, Spark developers hit roadblocks and could not optimize it any further. Finally, they decided to write the SQL Engine from scratch and that gave birth to Spark SQL.

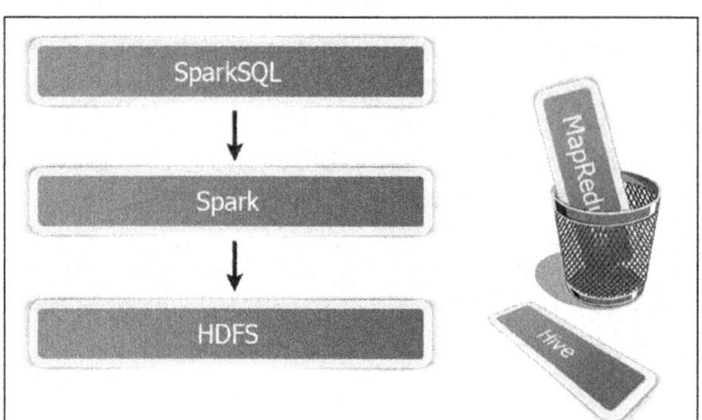

Spark SQL took care of all the performance challenges, but it had to provide compatibility with Hive and for that reason, a new wrapper context, `HiveContext`, was created on top of `SQLContext`.

Spark SQL supports accessing data using standard SQL queries and HiveQL, a SQL-like query language that Hive uses. In this chapter, we will explore different features of Spark SQL. It supports a subset of HiveQL as well as a subset of SQL 92. It runs SQL/HiveQL queries alongside, or replacing the existing Hive deployments.

Running SQL is only a part of the reason for the creation of Spark SQL. One big reason is that it helps to create and run Spark programs faster. It lets developers write less code, program read less data, and let the catalyst optimizer do all the heavy lifting.

Spark SQL uses a programming abstraction called **DataFrame**. It is a distributed collection of data organized in named columns. DataFrame is equivalent to a database table, but provides much finer level of optimization. The DataFrame API also ensures that Spark's performance is consistent across different language bindings.

Let's contrast DataFrames with RDDs. An RDD is an opaque collection of objects with no idea about the format of the underlying data. In contrast, DataFrames have schema associated with them. You can also look at DataFrames as RDDs with schema added to them. In fact, until Spark 1.2, there was an artifact called **SchemaRDD**, which has now evolved into DataFrame. They provide much richer functionality than SchemaRDDs.

This extra information about schema makes possible to do a lot of optimizations, which were not otherwise possible.

DataFrames also transparently load from various data sources, such as Hive tables, Parquet files, JSON files, and external databases using JDBC. DataFrames can be viewed as RDDs of row objects, allowing users to call the procedural Spark APIs such as map.

The DataFrame API is available in Scala, Java, Python, and also R starting Spark 1.4.

Users can perform relational operations on DataFrames using a **domain-specific language** (**DSL**). DataFrames support all the common relational operators and they all take expression objects in a limited DSL that lets Spark capture the structure of the expression.

We will start with the entry point into Spark SQL, that is, SQLContext. We will also cover HiveContext that is a wrapper around SQLContext to support Hive functionality. Please note that HiveContext is more battle-tested and provides a richer functionality, so it is strongly recommended to use it even if you do not plan to connect to Hive. Slowly, SQLContext will come to the same level of functionality as HiveContext is.

There are two ways to associate schema with RDDs to create DataFrames. The easy way is to leverage Scala case classes, which we are going to cover first. Spark uses Java reflection to deduce schema from case classes. There is also a way to programmatically specify schema for advanced needs, which we will cover next.

Spark SQL provides an easy way to both load and save the Parquet files, which will also be covered. Lastly, we will cover loading from and saving data to JSON.

Understanding the Catalyst optimizer

Most of the power of Spark SQL comes due to Catalyst optimizer, so it makes sense to spend some time understanding it.

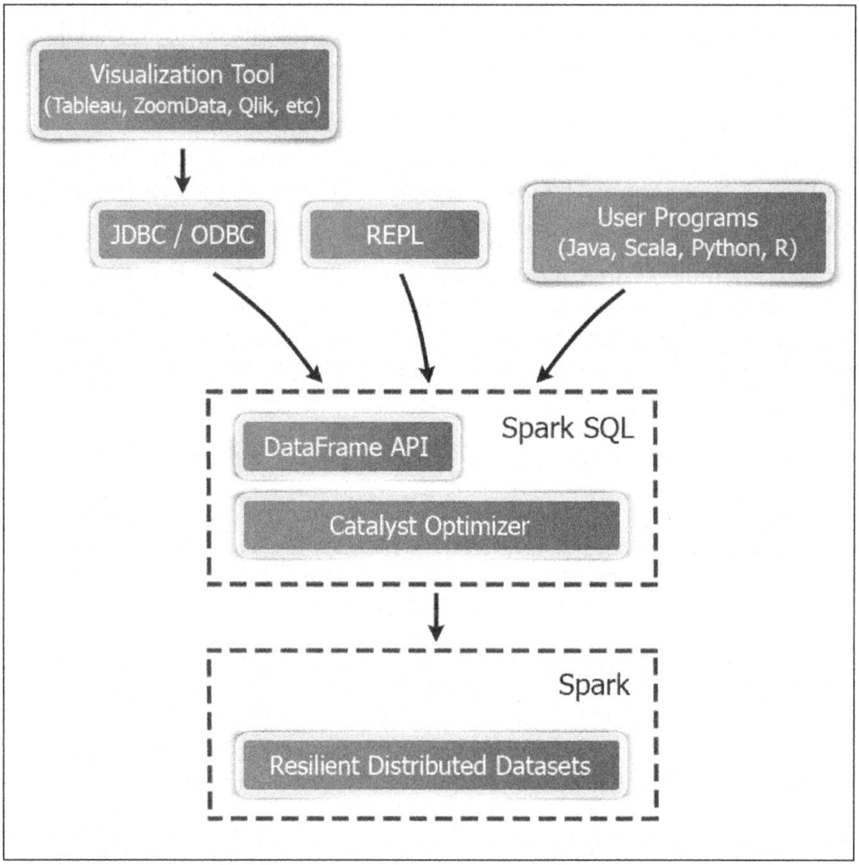

How it works...

Catalyst optimizer primarily leverages functional programming constructs of Scala such as pattern matching. It offers a general framework for transforming trees, which we use to perform analysis, optimization, planning, and runtime code generation.

Catalyst optimizer has two primary goals:

- Make adding new optimization techniques easy
- Enable external developers to extend the optimizer

Spark SQL uses Catalyst's transformation framework in four phases:

- Analyzing a logical plan to resolve references
- Logical plan optimization
- Physical planning
- Code generation to compile the parts of the query to Java bytecode

Analysis

The analysis phase involved looking at a SQL query or a DataFrame, creating a logical plan out of it, which is still unresolved (the columns referred may not exist or may be of wrong datatype) and then resolving this plan using the Catalog object (which connects to the physical data source), and creating a logical plan, as shown in the following diagram:

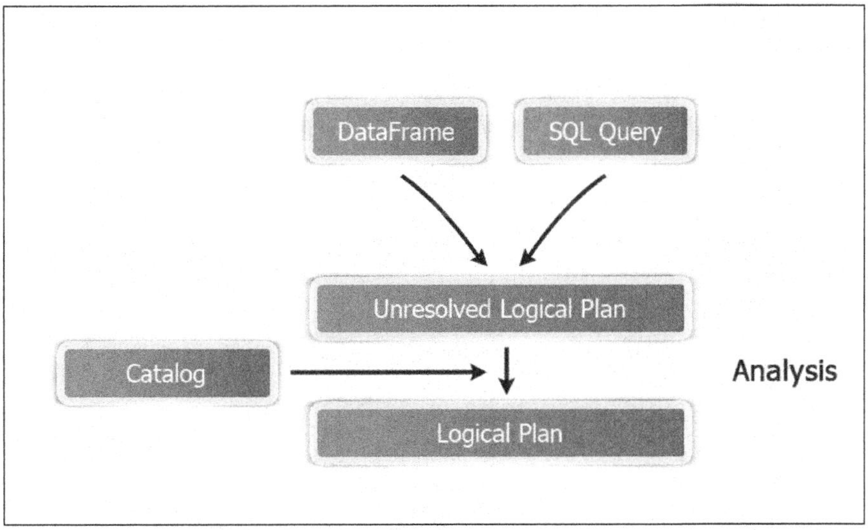

Logical plan optimization

The logical plan optimization phase applies standard rule-based optimization to the logical plan. These include constant folding, predicate pushdown, projection pruning, null propagation, Boolean expression simplification, and other rules.

I would like to draw special attention to predicate the pushdown rule here. The concept is simple; if you issue a query in one place to run against the massive data, which is another place, it can lead to a lot of unnecessary data moving across the network.

If we can push down the part of the query to where the data is stored, and thus filter out unnecessary data, it reduces network traffic significantly.

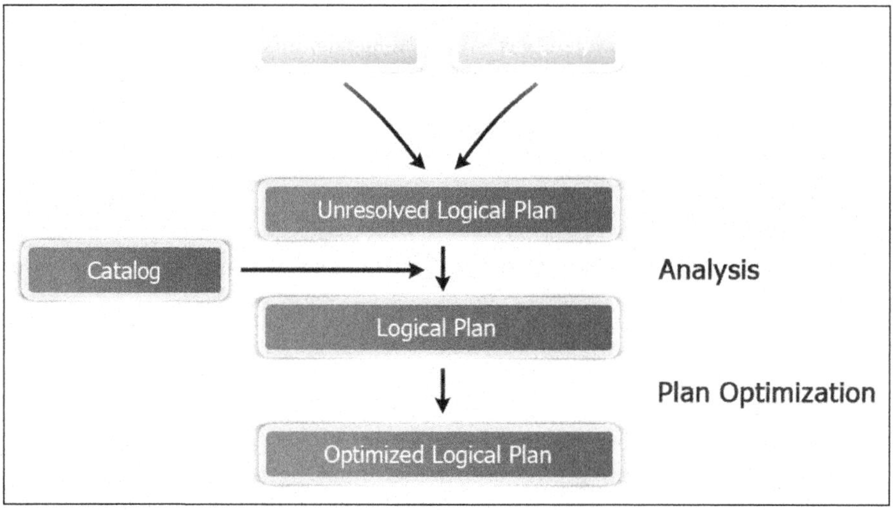

Physical planning

In the physical planning phase, Spark SQL takes a logical plan and generates one or more physical plans. It then measures the cost of each physical plan and generates one physical plan based on that.

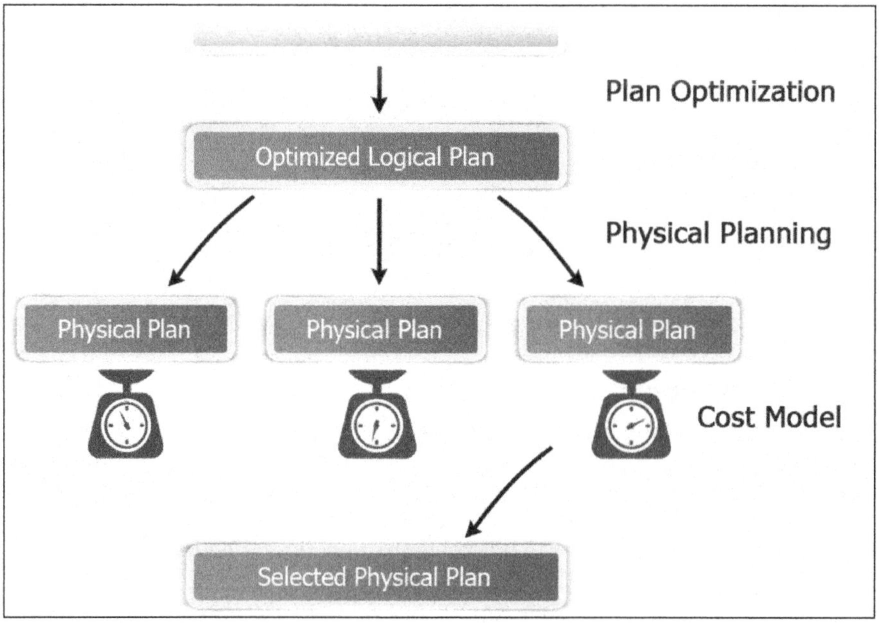

Code generation

The final phase of query optimization involves generating Java bytecode to run on each machine. It uses a special Scala feature called **Quasi quotes** to accomplish that.

Creating HiveContext

`SQLContext` and its descendant `HiveContext` are the two entry points into the world of Spark SQL. `HiveContext` provides a superset of functionality provided by SQLContext. The additional features are:

- More complete and battle-tested HiveQL parser
- Access to Hive UDFs
- Ability to read data from Hive tables

From Spark 1.3 onwards, the Spark shell comes loaded with sqlContext (which is an instance of `HiveContext` not `SQLContext`). If you are creating `SQLContext` in Scala code, it can be created using `SparkContext`, as follows:

```
val sc: SparkContext
val sqlContext = new org.apache.spark.sql.SQLContext(sc)
```

In this recipe, we will cover how to create instance of `HiveContext`, and then access Hive functionality through Spark SQL.

Getting ready

To enable Hive functionality, make sure that you have Hive enabled (-Phive) assembly JAR is available on all worker nodes; also, copy `hive-site.xml` into the `conf` directory of the Spark installation. It is important that Spark has access to `hive-site.xml`; otherwise, it will create its own Hive metastore and will not connect to your existing Hive warehouse.

By default, all the tables created by Spark SQL are Hive-managed tables, that is, Hive has complete control on life cycle of a table, including deleting it if table metadata is dropped using the `drop table` command. This holds true only for persistent tables. Spark SQL also has mechanism to create temporary tables out of DataFrames for ease of writing queries, and they are not managed by Hive.

Please note that Spark 1.4 supports Hive versions 0.13.1. You can specify a version of Hive you would like to build against using the `-Phive-<version> build` option while building with Maven. For example, to build with 0.12.0, you can use `-Phive-0.12.0`.

How to do it...

1. Start the Spark shell and give it some extra memory:

```
$ spark-shell --driver-memory 1G
```

2. Create an instance of `HiveContext`:

```
scala> val hc = new org.apache.spark.sql.hive.HiveContext(sc)
```

3. Create a Hive table `Person` with `first_name`, `last_name`, and `age` as columns:

```
scala>  hc.sql("create table if not exists person(first_name
string, last_name string, age int) row format delimited fields
terminated by ','")
```

4. Open another shell and create the `person` data in a local file:

```
$ mkdir person
$ echo "Barack,Obama,53" >> person/person.txt
$ echo "George,Bush,68" >> person/person.txt
$ echo "Bill,Clinton,68" >> person/person.txt
```

5. Load the data in the `person` table:

```
scala> hc.sql("load data local inpath \"/home/hduser/person\" into
table person")
```

6. Alternatively, load that data in the `person` table from HDFS:

```
scala> hc.sql("load data inpath \"/user/hduser/person\" into table
person")
```

> Please note that using `load data inpath` moves the data from another HDFS location to the Hive's `warehouse` directory, which is, by default, `/user/hive/warehouse`. You can also specify fully qualified path such as `hdfs://localhost:9000/user/hduser/person`.

7. Select the person data using HiveQL:

```
scala> val persons = hc.sql("from person select first_name,last_
name,age")
scala> persons.collect.foreach(println)
```

8. Create a new table from the output of a `select` query:

```
scala> hc.sql("create table person2 as select first_name, last_
name from person;")
```

9. You can also copy directly from one table to another:

```
scala> hc.sql("create table person2 like person location '/user/
hive/warehouse/person'")
```

10. Create two tables `people_by_last_name` and `people_by_age` to keep counts:

```
scala> hc.sql("create table people_by_last_name(last_name
string,count int)")
scala> hc.sql("create table people_by_age(age int,count int)")
```

11. You can also insert records into multiple tables using a HiveQL query:

```
scala> hc.sql("""from person
  insert overwrite table people_by_last_name
    select last_name, count(distinct first_name)
    group by last_name
insert overwrite table people_by_age
    select age, count(distinct first_name)
    group by age; """)
```

Inferring schema using case classes

Case classes are special classes in Scala that provide you with the boiler plate implementation of the constructor, getters (accessors), equals and hashCode, and implement `Serializable`. Case classes work really well to encapsulate data as objects. Readers, familiar with Java, can relate it to **plain old Java objects** (**POJOs**) or Java bean.

The beauty of case classes is that all that grunt work, which is required in Java, can be done with case classes in a single line of code. Spark uses reflection on case classes to infer schema.

How to do it...

1. Start the Spark shell and give it some extra memory:

```
$ spark-shell --driver-memory 1G
```

2. Import for the implicit conversions:

```
scala> import sqlContext.implicits._
```

3. Create a `Person` case class:

```
scala> case class Person(first_name:String,last_
name:String,age:Int)
```

4. In another shell, create some sample data to be put in HDFS:

```
$ mkdir person
$ echo "Barack,Obama,53" >> person/person.txt
$ echo "George,Bush,68" >> person/person.txt
$ echo "Bill,Clinton,68" >> person/person.txt
$ hdfs dfs -put person person
```

5. Load the `person` directory as an RDD:

```
scala> val p = sc.textFile("hdfs://localhost:9000/user/hduser/
person")
```

6. Split each line into an array of string, based on a comma, as a delimiter:

```
val pmap = p.map( line => line.split(","))
```

7. Convert the RDD of Array[String] into the RDD of `Person` case objects:

```
scala> val personRDD = pmap.map( p => Person(p(0),p(1),p(2).
toInt))
```

8. Convert the `personRDD` into the `personDF` DataFrame:

```
scala> val personDF = personRDD.toDF
```

9. Register the `personDF` as a table:

```
scala> personDF.registerTempTable("person")
```

10. Run a SQL query against it:

```
scala> val people = sql("select * from person")
```

11. Get the output values from `persons`:

```
scala> people.collect.foreach(println)
```

Programmatically specifying the schema

There are few cases where case classes might not work; one of these cases is that the case classes cannot take more than 22 fields. Another case can be that you do not know about schema beforehand. In this approach, the data is loaded as an RDD of the `Row` objects. Schema is created separately using the `StructType` and `StructField` objects, which represent a table and a field respectively. Schema is applied to the `Row` RDD to create a DataFrame.

How to do it...

1. Start the Spark shell and give it some extra memory:

```
$ spark-shell --driver-memory 1G
```

2. Import for the implicit conversion:

```
scala> import sqlContext.implicit._
```

3. Import the Spark SQL datatypes and `Row` objects:

```
scala> import org.apache.spark.sql._
scala> import org.apache.spark.sql.types._
```

4. In another shell, create some sample data to be put in HDFS:

```
$ mkdir person
$ echo "Barack,Obama,53" >> person/person.txt
$ echo "George,Bush,68" >> person/person.txt
$ echo "Bill,Clinton,68" >> person/person.txt
$ hdfs dfs -put person person
```

5. Load the `person` data in an RDD:

```
scala> val p = sc.textFile("hdfs://localhost:9000/user/hduser/
person")
```

6. Split each line into an array of string, based on a comma, as a delimiter:

```
scala> val pmap = p.map( line => line.split(","))
```

7. Convert the RDD of array[string] to the RDD of the `Row` objects:

```
scala> val personData = pmap.map( p => Row(p(0),p(1),p(2).toInt))
```

8. Create schema using the `StructType` and `StructField` objects. The `StructField` object takes parameters in the form of param name, param type, and nullability:

```
scala> val schema = StructType(
    Array(StructField("first_name",StringType,true),
StructField("last_name",StringType,true),
StructField("age",IntegerType,true)
))
```

9. Apply schema to create the `personDF` DataFrame:

```
scala> val personDF = sqlContext.createDataFrame(personData,sche
ma)
```

10. Register the `personDF` as a table:

```
scala> personDF.registerTempTable("person")
```

11. Run a SQL query against it:

```
scala> val persons = sql("select * from person")
```

12. Get the output values from `persons`:

```
scala> persons.collect.foreach(println)
```

In this recipe, we learned how to create a DataFrame by programmatically specifying schema.

How it works...

A `StructType` object defines the schema. You can consider it equivalent to a table or a row in the relational world. `StructType` takes in an array of the `StructField` objects, as in the following signature:

```
StructType(fields: Array[StructField])
```

A `StructField` object has the following signature:

```
StructField(name: String, dataType: DataType, nullable: Boolean =
true, metadata: Metadata = Metadata.empty)
```

Here is some more information on the parameters used:

- `name`: This represents the name of the field.
- `dataType`: This shows the datatype of this field.

  The following datatypes are allowed:

IntegerType	FloatType
BooleanType	ShortType
LongType	ByteType
DoubleType	StringType

- `nullable`: This shows whether this field can be null.
- `metadata`: This shows the metadata of this field. Metadata is a wrapper over `Map[String,Any]` so that it can contain any arbitrary metadata.

Loading and saving data using the Parquet format

Apache Parquet is a columnar data storage format, specifically designed for big data storage and processing. Parquet is based on record shredding and assembly algorithm in the Google Dremel paper. In Parquet, data in a single column is stored contiguously.

The columnar format gives Parquet some unique benefits. For example, if you have a table with 100 columns and you mostly access 10 columns, in a row-based format you will have to load all 100 columns, as granularity level is at row level. But, in Parquet, you will only load 10 columns. Another benefit is that since all the data in a given column is of the same datatype (by definition), compression is much more efficient.

How to do it...

1. Open the terminal and create the `person` data in a local file:

   ```
   $ mkdir person
   $ echo "Barack,Obama,53" >> person/person.txt
   $ echo "George,Bush,68" >> person/person.txt
   $ echo "Bill,Clinton,68" >> person/person.txt
   ```

2. Upload the `person` directory to HDFS:

   ```
   $ hdfs dfs -put person /user/hduser/person
   ```

3. Start the Spark shell and give it some extra memory:

   ```
   $ spark-shell --driver-memory 1G
   ```

4. Import for the implicit conversion:

   ```
   scala> import sqlContext.implicits._
   ```

5. Create a case class for `Person`:

   ```
   scala> case class Person(firstName: String, lastName: String,
   age:Int)
   ```

6. Load the `person` directory from HDFS and map it to the `Person` case class:

   ```
   scala> val personRDD = sc.textFile("hdfs://localhost:9000/user/
   hduser/person").map(_.split("\t")).map(p => Person(p(0),p(1),p(2).
   toInt))
   ```

7. Convert the `personRDD` into the `person` DataFrame:

   ```
   scala> val person = personRDD.toDF
   ```

8. Register the `person` DataFrame as a temp table so that SQL queries can be run against it. Please note that the DataFrame name does not have to be the same as the table name.

```
scala> person.registerTempTable("person")
```

9. Select all the person with age over 60 years:

```
scala> val sixtyPlus = sql("select * from person where age > 60")
```

10. Print values:

```
scala> sixtyPlus.collect.foreach(println)
```

11. Let's save this `sixtyPlus` RDD in the Parquet format:

```
scala> sixtyPlus.saveAsParquetFile("hdfs://localhost:9000/user/
hduser/sp.parquet")
```

12. The previous step created a directory called `sp.parquet` in the HDFS root. You can run the `hdfs dfs -ls` command in another shell to make sure that it's created:

```
$ hdfs dfs -ls sp.parquet
```

13. Load contents of the Parquet files in the Spark shell:

```
scala> val parquetDF = sqlContext.load("hdfs://localhost:9000/
user/hduser/sp.parquet")
```

14. Register the loaded `parquet` DF as a `temp` table:

```
scala> parquetDF.registerTempTable("sixty_plus")
```

15. Run a query against the preceding `temp` table:

```
scala> sql("select * from sixty_plus")
```

How it works...

Let's spend some time understanding the Parquet format deeper. The following is sample data represented in the table format:

First_Name	Last_Name	Age
Barack	Obama	53
George	Bush	68
Bill	Clinton	68

In the row format, the data will be stored like this:

Barack	Obama	53	George	Bush	68	Bill	Clinton	68

In the columnar layout, the data will be stored like this:

Row group =>	Barack	George	Bill	Obama	Bush	Clinton	53	68	68
	Column chunk			Column chunk			Column chunk		

Here's a brief description about the different parts:

- **Row group**: This shows the horizontal partitioning of data into rows. A row group consists of column chunks.
- **Column chunk**: A column chunk has data for a given column in a row group. A column chunk is always physically contiguous. A row group has only one column chunk per column.
- **Page**: A column chunk is divided into pages. A page is a unit of storage and cannot be further divided. Pages are written back to back in column chunk. The data for a page can be compressed.

If there is already data in a Hive table, say, the `person` table, you can directly save it in the Parquet format by performing the following steps:

1. Create a table named `person_parquet` with schema, the same as `person`, but in the Parquet storage format (for Hive 0.13 onwards):

```
hive> create table person_parquet like person stored as parquet
```

2. Insert data in the `person_parquet` table by importing it from the `person` table:

```
hive> insert overwrite table person_parquet select * from person;
```

> Sometimes, data imported from other sources, such as Impala, saves string as binary. To convert it to string while reading, set the following property in `SparkConf`:
>
> ```
> scala> sqlContext.setConf("spark.sql.parquet.
> binaryAsString","true")
> ```

There's more...

If you are using Spark 1.4 or later, there is a new interface both to write to and read from Parquet. To write the data to Parquet (step 11 rewritten), let's save this `sixtyPlus` RDD to the Parquet format (RDD implicitly gets converted to DataFrame):

```
scala>sixtyPlus.write.parquet("hdfs://localhost:9000/user/hduser/
sp.parquet")
```

To read from Parquet (step 13 rewritten; the result is DataFrame), load the contents of the Parquet files in the Spark shell:

```
scala>val parquetDF = sqlContext.read.parquet("hdfs://
localhost:9000/user/hduser/sp.parquet")
```

Loading and saving data using the JSON format

JSON is a lightweight data-interchange format. It is based on a subset of the JavaScript programming language. JSON's popularity is directly related to XML getting unpopular. XML was a great solution to provide a structure to the data in a plain text format. With time, XML documents became more and more heavy and the overhead was not worth it.

JSON solved this problem by providing structure with minimal overhead. Some people call JSON **fat-free XML**.

The JSON syntax follows these rules:

- Data is in the form of key-value pairs:

  `"firstName" : "Bill"`

- There are four datatypes in JSON:
  - String ("firstName" : "Barack")
  - Number ("age" : 53)
  - Boolean ("alive": true)
  - null ("manager" : null)
- Data is delimited by commas
- Curly braces {} represents an object:

  `{ "firstName" : "Bill", "lastName": "Clinton", "age": 68 }`

- Square brackets [] represent an array:

  ```
  [{ "firstName" : "Bill", "lastName": "Clinton", "age": 68
  },{"firstName": "Barack","lastName": "Obama", "age": 43}]
  ```

In this recipe, we will explore how to save and load it in the JSON format.

How to do it...

1. Open the terminal and create the `person` data in the JSON format:

```
$ mkdir jsondata
$ vi jsondata/person.json
{"first_name" : "Barack", "last_name" : "Obama", "age" : 53}
{"first_name" : "George", "last_name" : "Bush", "age" : 68 }
{"first_name" : "Bill", "last_name" : "Clinton", "age" : 68 }
```

2. Upload the `jsondata` directory to HDFS:

```
$ hdfs dfs -put jsondata /user/hduser/jsondata
```

3. Start the Spark shell and give it some extra memory:

```
$ spark-shell --driver-memory 1G
```

4. Create an instance of `SQLContext`:

```
scala> val sqlContext = new org.apache.spark.sql.SQLContext(sc)
```

5. Import for the implicit conversion:

```
scala> import sqlContext.implicits._
```

6. Load the `jsondata` directory from HDFS:

```
scala> val person = sqlContext.jsonFile("hdfs://localhost:9000/
user/hduser/jsondata")
```

7. Register the `person` DF as a `temp` table so that the SQL queries can be run against it:

```
scala> person.registerTempTable("person")
```

8. Select all the persons with age over 60 years:

```
scala> val sixtyPlus = sql("select * from person where age > 60")
```

9. Print values:

```
scala> sixtyPlus.collect.foreach(println)
```

10. Let's save this `sixtyPlus` DF in the JSON format

```
scala> sixtyPlus.toJSON.saveAsTextFile("hdfs://localhost:9000/
user/hduser/sp")
```

11. Last step created a directory called `sp` in the HDFS root. You can run the `hdfs dfs -ls` command in another shell to make sure it's created:

```
$ hdfs dfs -ls sp
```

How it works...

The `sc.jsonFile` internally uses `TextInputFormat`, which processes one line at a time. Therefore, one JSON record cannot be on multiple lines. It would be a valid JSON format if you use multiple lines, but it will not work with Spark and will throw an exception.

It is allowed to have more than one object in a line. For example, you can have the information of two persons in one line as an array, as follows:

```
[{"firstName":"Barack", "lastName":"Obama"},{"firstName":"Bill",
"lastName":"Clinton"}]
```

This recipe concludes saving and loading data in the JSON format using Spark.

There's more...

If you are using Spark Version 1.4 or later, `SqlContext` provides an easier interface to load the `jsondata` directory from HDFS:

```
scala> val person = sqlContext.read.json ("hdfs://localhost:9000/
user/hduser/jsondata")
```

The `sqlContext.jsonFile` is deprecated in version 1.4, and `sqlContext.read.json` is the recommend approach.

Loading and saving data from relational databases

In the previous chapter, we learned how to load data from a relational data into an RDD using JdbcRDD. Spark 1.4 has support to load data directly into Dataframe from a JDBC resource. This recipe will explore how to do it.

Getting ready

Please make sure that JDBC driver JAR is visible on the client node and all the slaves nodes on which executor will run.

How to do it...

1. Create a table named `person` in MySQL using the following DDL:

```
CREATE TABLE 'person' (
  'person_id' int(11) NOT NULL AUTO_INCREMENT,
  'first_name' varchar(30) DEFAULT NULL,
```

```
    'last_name' varchar(30) DEFAULT NULL,
    'gender' char(1) DEFAULT NULL,
    'age' tinyint(4) DEFAULT NULL,
    PRIMARY KEY ('person_id')
  )
```

2. Insert some data:

```
Insert into person values('Barack','Obama','M',53);
Insert into person values('Bill','Clinton','M',71);
Insert into person values('Hillary','Clinton','F',68);
Insert into person values('Bill','Gates','M',69);
Insert into person values('Michelle','Obama','F',51);
```

3. Download `mysql-connector-java-x.x.xx-bin.jar` from `http://dev.mysql.com/downloads/connector/j/`.
4. Make MySQL driver available to the Spark shell and launch it:

```
$ spark-shell --driver-class-path/path-to-mysql-jar/mysql-connector-java-5.1.34-bin.jar
```

> Please note that `path-to-mysql-jar` is not the actual path name. You need to use your path name.

5. Construct a JDBC URL:

```
scala> val url="jdbc:mysql://localhost:3306/hadoopdb"
```

6. Create a connection properties object with username and password:

```
scala> val prop = new java.util.Properties
scala> prop.setProperty("user","hduser")
scala> prop.setProperty("password","********")
```

7. Load DataFrame with JDBC data source (url, table name, properties):

```
      scala> val people = sqlContext.read.jdbc(url,"person",prop)
```

8. Show the results in a nice tabular format by executing the following command:

```
scala> people.show
```

9. This has loaded the whole table. What if I only would like to load males (url, table name, predicates, properties)? To do this, run the following command:

```
scala> val males = sqlContext.read.jdbc(url,"person",Array("gender='M'"),prop)
scala> males.show
```

10. Show only first names by executing the following command:

```
scala> val first_names = people.select("first_name")
scala> first_names.show
```

11. Show only people below age 60 by executing the following command:

```
scala> val below60 = people.filter(people("age") < 60)
scala> below60.show
```

12. Group people by gender as follows:

```
scala> val grouped = people.groupBy("gender")
```

13. Find the number of males and females by executing the following command:

```
scala> val gender_count = grouped.count
scala> gender_count.show
```

14. Find the average age of males and females by executing the following command:

```
scala> val avg_age = grouped.avg("age")
scala> avg_age.show
```

15. Now if you'd like to save this `avg_age` data to a new table, run the following command:

```
scala> gender_count.write.jdbc(url,"gender_count",prop)
```

16. Save the people DataFrame in the Parquet format:

```
scala> people.write.parquet("people.parquet")
```

17. Save the people DataFrame in the JSON format:

```
scala> people.write.json("people.json")
```

Loading and saving data from an arbitrary source

So far, we have covered three data sources that are inbuilt with DataFrames—`parquet` (default), `json`, and `jdbc`. Dataframes are not limited to these three and can load and save to any arbitrary data source by specifying the format manually.

In this recipe, we will cover loading and saving data from arbitrary sources.

How to do it...

1. Start the Spark shell and give it some extra memory:

```
$ spark-shell --driver-memory 1G
```

2. Load the data from Parquet; since `parquet` is the default data source, you do not have to specify it:

```
scala> val people = sqlContext.read.load("hdfs://localhost:9000/
user/hduser/people.parquet")
```

3. Load the data from Parquet by manually specifying the format:

```
scala> val people = sqlContext.read.format("org.apache.spark.sql.
parquet").load("hdfs://localhost:9000/user/hduser/people.parquet")
```

4. For inbuilt datatypes (`parquet`,`json`, and `jdbc`), you do not have to specify the full format name, only specifying `"parquet"`, `"json"`, or `"jdbc"` works:

```
scala> val people = sqlContext.read.format("parquet").
load("hdfs://localhost:9000/user/hduser/people.parquet")
```

> When writing data, there are four save modes: `append`, `overwrite`, `errorIfExists`, and `ignore`. The `append` mode adds data to data source, `overwrite` overwrites it, `errorIfExists` throws an exception that data already exists, and `ignore` does nothing when data already exists.

5. Save people as JSON in the `append` mode:

```
scala> val people = people.write.format("json").mode("append").
save ("hdfs://localhost:9000/user/hduser/people.json")
```

There's more...

The Spark SQL's data source API saves to a variety of data sources. To find more information, visit `http://spark-packages.org/`.

5
Spark Streaming

Spark Streaming adds the holy grail of big data processing—that is, real-time analytics—to Apache Spark. It enables Spark to ingest live data streams and provides real-time intelligence at a very low latency of a few seconds.

In this chapter, we'll cover the following recipes:

- Word count using Streaming
- Streaming Twitter data
- Streaming using Kafka

Introduction

Streaming is the process of dividing continuously flowing input data into discreet units so that it can be processed easily. Familiar examples in real life are streaming video and audio content (though a user can download the full movie before he/she can watch it, a faster solution is to stream data in small chunks that start playing for the user while the rest of the data is being downloaded in the background).

Real-world examples of streaming, besides multimedia, are the processing of market feeds, weather data, electronic stock trading data, and so on. All of these applications produce large volumes of data at very fast rates and require special handling of the data so that insights can be derived from data in real time.

Streaming has a few basic concepts, which are better to understand before we focus on Spark Streaming. The rate at which a streaming application receives data is called **data rate** and is expressed in the form of **kilobytes per second** (**kbps**) or **megabytes per second** (**mbps**).

One important use case of streaming is **complex event processing** (**CEP**). In CEP, it is important to control the scope of the data being processed. This scope is called window, which can be either based on time or size. An example of a time-based window is to analyze data that has come in last one minute. An example of a size-based window can be the average ask price of the last 100 trades of a given stock.

Spark Streaming is Spark's library that provides support to process live data. This stream can come from any source, such as Twitter, Kafka, or Flume.

Spark Streaming has a few fundamental building blocks that we need to understand well before diving into the recipes.

Spark Streaming has a context wrapper called `StreamingContext`, which wraps around `SparkContext` and is the entry point to the Spark Streaming functionality. Streaming data, by definition, is continuous and needs to be time-sliced to process. This slice of time is called the **batch interval**, which is specified when `StreamingContext` is created. There is one-to-one mapping of RDD and batch, that is, each batch results in one RDD. As you can see in the following image, Spark Streaming takes continuous data, break it into batches and feed to Spark.

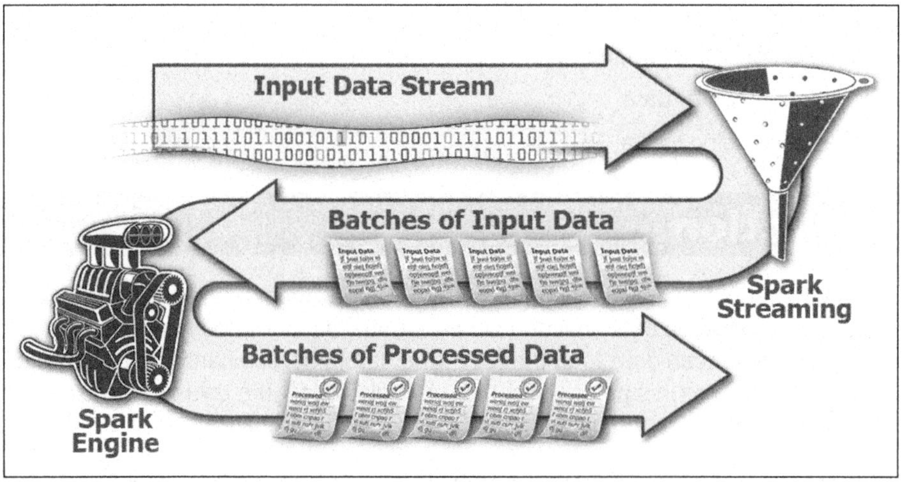

Batch interval is important to optimize your streaming application. Ideally, you want to process data at least as fast as it is getting ingested; otherwise, your application will develop a backlog. Spark Streaming collects data for the duration of a batch interval, say, 2 seconds. The moment this 2 second interval is over, data collected in that interval will be given to Spark for processing and Streaming will focus on collecting data for the next batch interval. Now, this 2 second batch interval is all Spark has to process data, as it should be free to receive data from the next batch. If Spark can process the data faster, you can reduce the batch interval to, say, 1 second. If Spark is not able to keep up with this speed, you have to increase the batch interval.

The continuous stream of RDDs in Spark Streaming needs to be represented in the form of an abstraction through which it can be processed. This abstraction is called **Discretized Stream** (**DStream**). Any operation applied on DStream results in an operation on underlying RDDs.

Every input DStream is associated with a receiver (except for file stream). A receiver receives data from the input source and stores it in Spark's memory. There are two types of streaming sources:

- Basic sources, such as file and socket connections
- Advanced sources, such as Kafka and Flume

Spark Streaming also provides windowed computations in which you can apply the transformation over a sliding window of data. A sliding window operation is based on two parameters:

- **Window length**: This is the duration of the window. For example, if you want to get analytics of the last 1 minute of data, the window length will be 1 minute.
- **Sliding interval**: This depicts how frequently you want to perform an operation. Say you want to perform the operation every 10 seconds; this means that every 10 seconds, 1 minute of window will have 50 seconds of data common with the last window and 10 seconds of the new data.

Both these parameters work on underlying RDDs that, obviously, cannot be broken apart; therefore, both of these should be a multiple of the batch interval. The window length has to be a multiple of the sliding interval as well.

DStream also has output operations, which allow data to be pushed to external systems. They are similar to actions on RDDs (one higher level of abstraction of what you do at DStream happens to RDDs).

Besides print to print content of DStream, standard RDD actions, such as `saveAsTextFile`, `saveAsObjectFile`, and `saveAsHadoopFile`, are supported by similar counterparts, such as `saveAsTextFiles`, `saveAsObjectFiles`, and `saveAsHadoopFiles`, respectively.

One very useful output operation is `foreachRDD(func)`, which applies any arbitrary function to all the RDDs.

Word count using Streaming

Let's start with a simple example of Streaming in which in one terminal, we will type some text and the Streaming application will capture it in another window.

How to do it...

1. Start the Spark shell and give it some extra memory:

```
$ spark-shell --driver-memory 1G
```

2. Stream specific imports:

```
scala> import org.apache.spark.SparkConf
scala> import org.apache.spark.streaming.{Seconds,
StreamingContext}
scala> import org.apache.spark.storage.StorageLevel
scala> import StorageLevel._
```

3. Import for an implicit conversion:

```
scala> import org.apache.spark._
scala> import org.apache.spark.streaming._
scala> import org.apache.spark.streaming.StreamingContext._
```

4. Create `StreamingContext` with a 2 second batch interval:

```
scala> val ssc = new StreamingContext(sc, Seconds(2))
```

5. Create a `SocketTextStream` Dstream on localhost with port `8585` with the `MEMORY_ONLY` caching:

```
scala> val lines = ssc.socketTextStream("localhost",8585,MEMORY_
ONLY)
```

6. Divide the lines into multiple words:

```
scala> val wordsFlatMap = lines.flatMap(_.split(" "))
```

7. Convert word to (word,1), that is, output `1` as the value for each occurrence of a word as the key:

```
scala> val wordsMap = wordsFlatMap.map( w => (w,1))
```

8. Use the `reduceByKey` method to add a number of occurrences for each word as the key (the function works on two consecutive values at a time, represented by `a` and `b`):

```
scala> val wordCount = wordsMap.reduceByKey( (a,b) => (a+b))
```

9. Print `wordCount`:

```
scala> wordCount.print
```

10. Start `StreamingContext`; remember, nothing happens until `StreamingContext` is started:

```
scala> ssc.start
```

11. Now, in a separate window, start the netcat server:

```
$ nc -lk 8585
```

12. Enter different lines, such as `to be or not to be`:

```
to be or not to be
```

13. Check the Spark shell, and you will see word count results like the following screenshot:

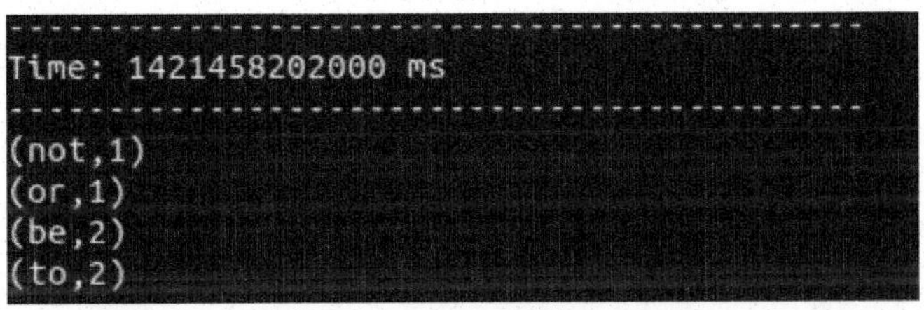

Streaming Twitter data

Twitter is a famous microblogging platform. It produces a massive amount of data with around 500 million tweets sent each day. Twitter allows its data to be accessed by APIs and that makes it the poster child of testing any big data streaming application.

In this recipe, we will see how we can live stream data in Spark using Twitter streaming libraries. Twitter is just one source of providing the streaming data to Spark and has no special status. Therefore, there are no built-in libraries for Twitter. Spark does provide some APIs to facilitate integration with Twitter libraries, though.

An example use of live Twitter data feed can be to find trending tweets in the last 5 minutes.

How to do it...

1. Create a Twitter account if you do not already have one.
2. Go to `http://apps.twitter.com`.
3. Click on **Create New App**.
4. Enter **Name**, **Description**, **Website**, and **Callback URL**, and then click on **Create your Twitter Application**.

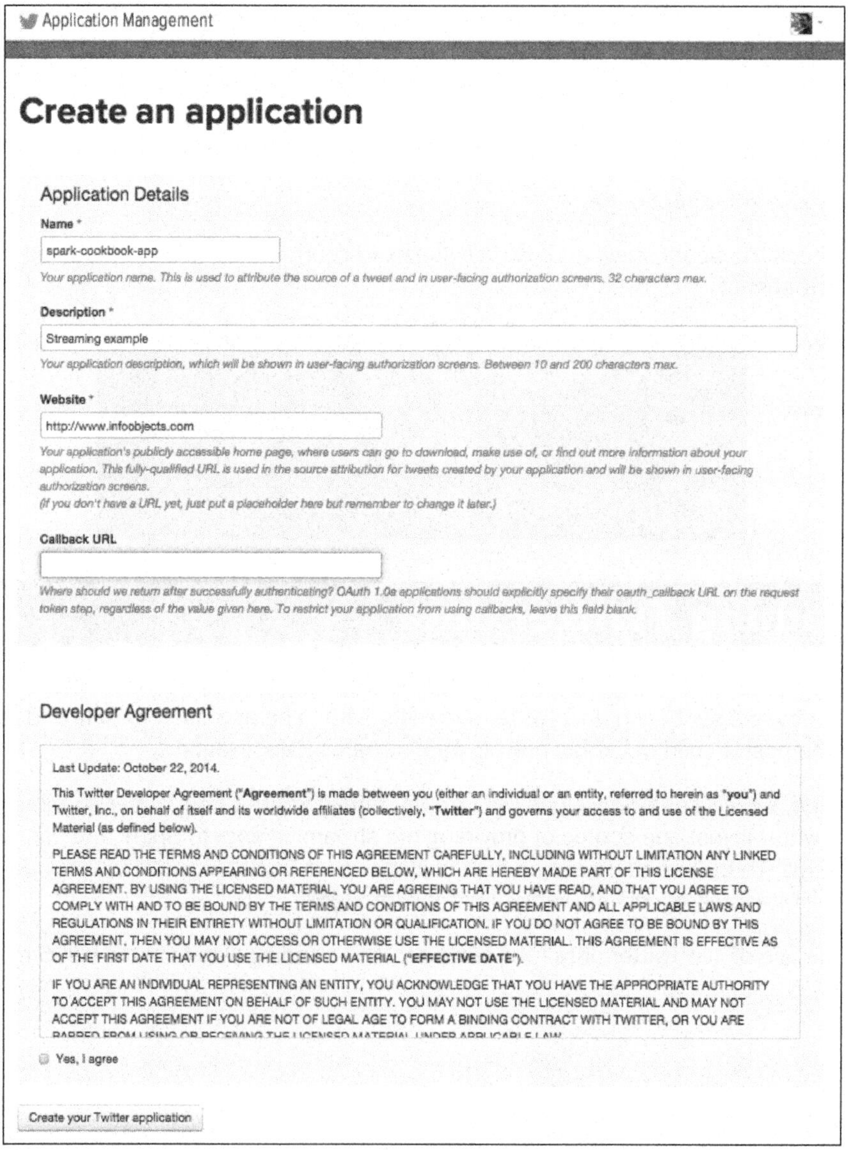

5. You will reach **Application Management** screen.
6. Navigate to **Keys and Access Tokens** | **Create my access Token**.

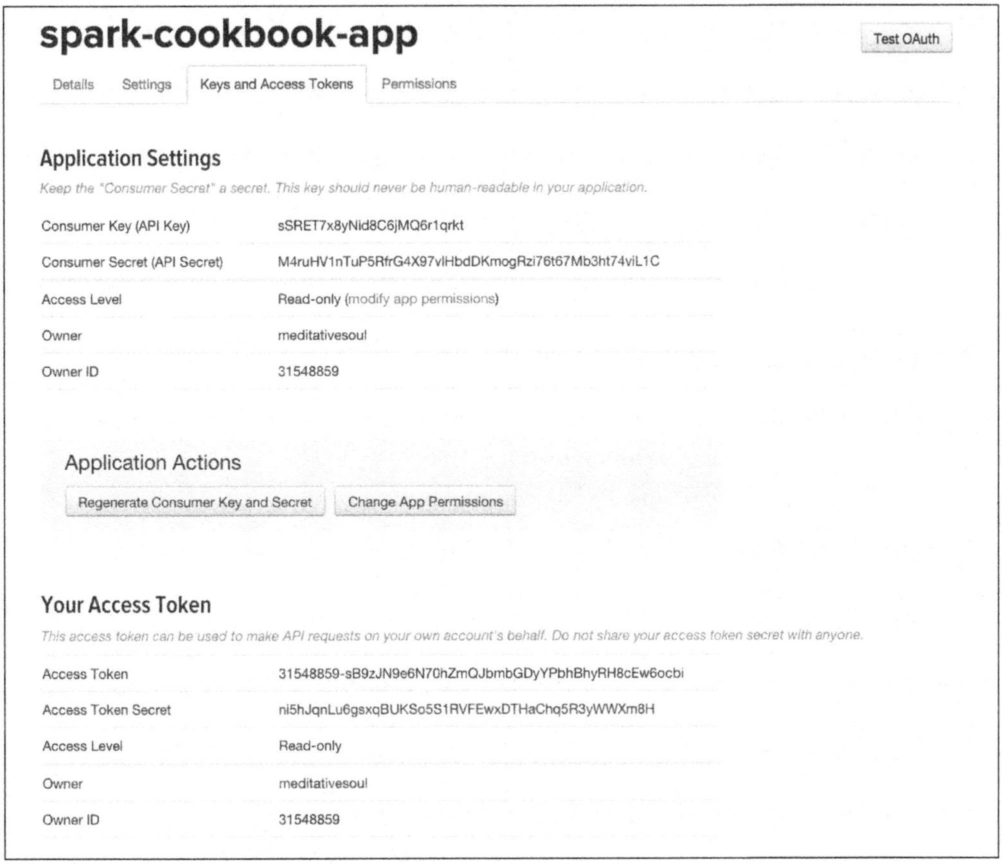

7. Note down the four values in this screen that we will use in step 14:

   Consumer Key (API Key)

   Consumer Secret (API Secret)

   Access Token

   Access Token Secret

8. We will need to provide the values in this screen in some time, but, for now, let's download the third-party libraries needed from Maven central:

```
$ wget http://central.maven.org/maven2/org/apache/spark/spark-streaming-twitter_2.10/1.2.0/spark-streaming-twitter_2.10-1.2.0.jar
```

```
$ wget http://central.maven.org/maven2/org/twitter4j/twitter4j-stream/4.0.2/twitter4j-stream-4.0.2.jar
```

```
$ wget http://central.maven.org/maven2/org/twitter4j/twitter4j-
core/4.0.2/twitter4j-core-4.0.2.jar
```

9. Open the Spark shell, supplying the preceding three JARS as the dependency:

```
$ spark-shell --jars spark-streaming-twitter_2.10-1.2.0.jar,
twitter4j-stream-4.0.2.jar,twitter4j-core-4.0.2.jar
```

10. Perform imports that are Twitter-specific:

```
scala> import org.apache.spark.streaming.twitter._
scala> import twitter4j.auth._
scala> import twitter4j.conf._
```

11. Stream specific imports:

```
scala> import org.apache.spark.streaming.{Seconds,
StreamingContext}
```

12. Import for an implicit conversion:

```
scala> import org.apache.spark._
scala> import org.apache.spark.streaming._
scala> import org.apache.spark.streaming.StreamingContext._
```

13. Create `StreamingContext` with a 10 second batch interval:

```
scala> val ssc = new StreamingContext(sc, Seconds(10))
```

14. Create `StreamingContext` with a 2 second batch interval:

```
scala> val cb = new ConfigurationBuilder
scala> cb.setDebugEnabled(true)
.setOAuthConsumerKey("FKNryYEKeCrKzGV7zuZW4EKeN")
.setOAuthConsumerSecret("x6Y0zcTBOwVxpvekSCnGzbi3NYN
rM5b8ZMZRIPI1XRC3pDyOs1")
  .setOAuthAccessToken("31548859-DHbESdk6YoghCLcfhMF8
8QEFDvEjxbM6Q90eoZTGl")
.setOAuthAccessTokenSecret("wjcWPvtejZSbp9cgLejUdd6W1
MJqFzm5lByUFZl1NYgrV")
val auth = new OAuthAuthorization(cb.build)
```

> These are sample values and you should put your own values.

15. Create Twitter DStream:

```
scala> val tweets = TwitterUtils.createStream(ssc,auth)
```

16. Filter out English tweets:

```
scala> val englishTweets = tweets.filter(_.getLang()=="en")
```

17. Get text out of the tweets:

```
scala> val status = englishTweets.map(status => status.getText)
```

18. Set the checkpoint directory:

```
scala> ssc.checkpoint("hdfs://localhost:9000/user/hduser/
checkpoint")
```

19. Start `StreamingContext`:

```
scala> ssc.start
scala> ssc.awaitTermination
```

20. You can put all these commands together using `:paste`:

```
scala> :paste
import org.apache.spark.streaming.twitter._
import twitter4j.auth._
import twitter4j.conf._
import org.apache.spark.streaming.{Seconds, StreamingContext}
import org.apache.spark._
import org.apache.spark.streaming._
import org.apache.spark.streaming.StreamingContext._
val ssc = new StreamingContext(sc, Seconds(10))
val cb = new ConfigurationBuilder
cb.setDebugEnabled(true).setOAuthConsumerKey("FKNryYEKe
CrKzGV7zuZW4EKeN")
  .setOAuthConsumerSecret("x6Y0zcTBOwVxpvekSCnGzbi3NYNr
M5b8ZMZRIPI1XRC3pDyOs1")
  .setOAuthAccessToken("31548859-DHbESdk6YoghCLcfhMF88Q
EFDvEjxbM6Q90eoZTGl")
  .setOAuthAccessTokenSecret("wjcWPvtejZSbp9cgLejUdd6W1
MJqFzm5lByUFZl1NYgrV")
val auth = new OAuthAuthorization(cb.build)
val tweets = TwitterUtils.createStream(ssc,Some(auth))
val englishTweets = tweets.filter(_.getLang()=="en")
val status = englishTweets.map(status => status.getText)
status.print
ssc.checkpoint("hdfs://localhost:9000/checkpoint")
ssc.start
ssc.awaitTermination
```

Streaming using Kafka

Kafka is a distributed, partitioned, and replicated commit log service. In simple words, it is a distributed messaging server. Kafka maintains the message feed in categories called **topics**. An example of the topic can be a ticker symbol of a company you would like to get news about, for example, CSCO for Cisco.

Processes that produce messages are called **producers** and those that consume messages are called **consumers**. In traditional messaging, the messaging service has one central messaging server, also called **broker**. Since Kafka is a distributed messaging service, it has a cluster of brokers, which functionally act as one Kafka broker, as shown here:

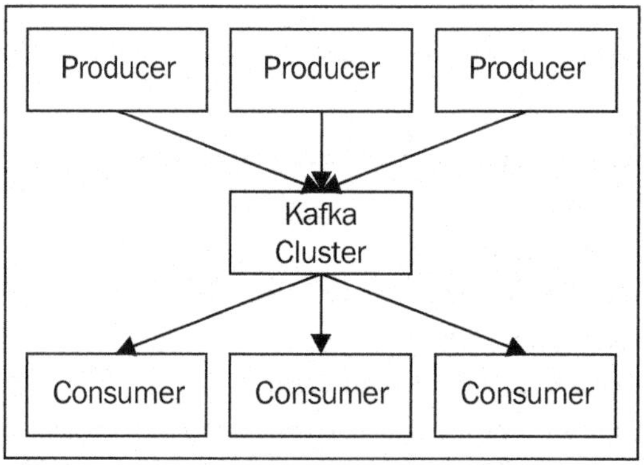

For each topic, Kafka maintains the partitioned log. This partitioned log consists of one or more partitions spread across the cluster, as shown in the following figure:

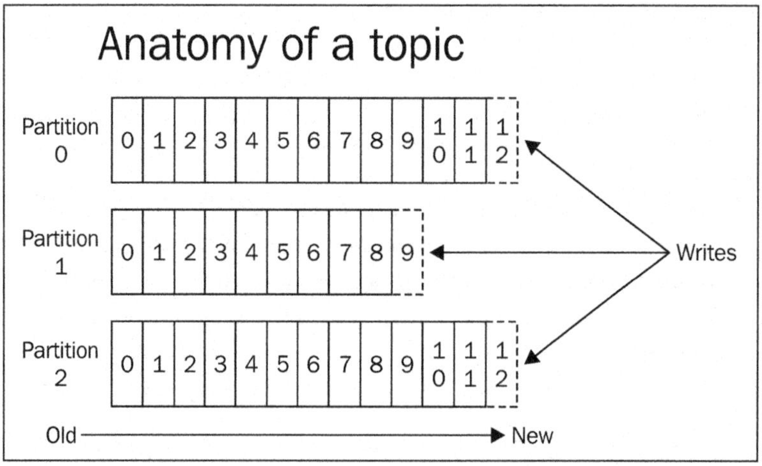

Kafka borrows a lot of concepts from Hadoop and other big data frameworks. The concept of partition is very similar to the concept of `InputSplit` in Hadoop. In the simplest form, while using `TextInputFormat`, an `InputSplit` is same as a block. A block is read in the form of a key-value pair in `TextInputFormat`, where the key is the byte offset of a line and the value is content of the line itself. In a similar way, in a Kafka partition, records are stored and retrieved in the form of key-value pairs, where the key is a sequential ID number called the offset and the value is the actual message.

In Kafka, message retention does not depend on the consumption by a consumer. Messages are retained for a configurable period of time. Each consumer is free to read messages in any order they like. All it needs to retain is an offset. Another analogy can be reading a book in which the page number is analogous to the offset, while the page content is analogous to the message. The reader is free to read whichever way he/she wants as long as they remember the bookmark (the current offset).

To provide functionality similar to pub/sub and PTP (queues) in traditional messaging systems, Kafka has the concept of consumer groups. A consumer group is a group of consumers, which the Kafka cluster treats as a single unit. In a consumer group, only one consumer needs to receive a message. If consumer C1, in the following diagram, receives the first message for topic T1, all the following messages on that topic will also be delivered to this consumer. Using this strategy, Kafka guarantees the order of message delivery for a given topic.

In extreme cases, when all consumers are in one consumer group, the Kafka cluster acts like PTP/queue. In another extreme case, if every consumer belongs to a different group, it acts like pub/sub. In practice, each consumer group has a limited number of consumers.

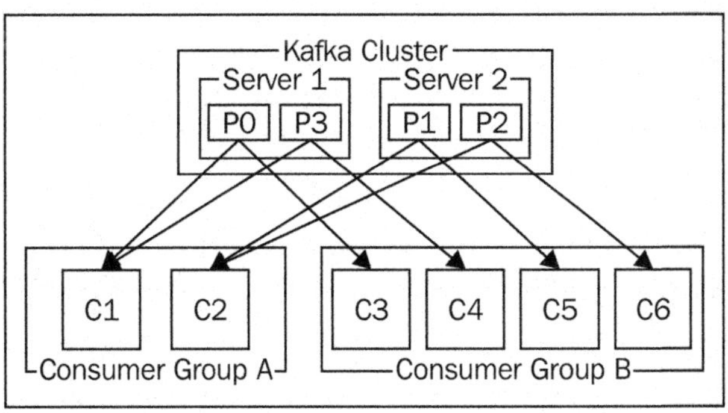

This recipe will show you how to perform a word count using data coming from Kafka.

Getting ready

This recipe assumes Kafka is already installed. Kafka comes with ZooKeeper bundled. We are assuming Kafka's home is in `/opt/infoobjects/kafka`:

1. Start ZooKeeper:

   ```
   $ /opt/infoobjects/kafka/bin/zookeeper-server-start.sh /opt/
   infoobjects/kafka/config/zookeeper.properties
   ```

2. Start the Kafka server:

   ```
   $ /opt/infoobjects/kafka/bin/kafka-server-start.sh /opt/
   infoobjects/kafka/config/server.properties
   ```

3. Create a `test` topic:

   ```
   $ /opt/infoobjects/kafka/bin/kafka-topics.sh --create --zookeeper
   localhost:2181 --replication-factor 1 --partitions 1 --topic test
   ```

How to do it...

1. Download the `spark-streaming-kafka` library and its dependencies:

   ```
   $ wget http://central.maven.org/maven2/org/apache/spark/spark-
   streaming-kafka_2.10/1.2.0/spark-streaming-kafka_2.10-1.2.0.jar
   $ wget http://central.maven.org/maven2/org/apache/kafka/
   kafka_2.10/0.8.1/kafka_2.10-0.8.1.jar
   $ wget http://central.maven.org/maven2/com/yammer/metrics/metrics-
   core/2.2.0/metrics-core-2.2.0.jar
   $ wget http://central.maven.org/maven2/com/101tec/zkclient/0.4/
   zkclient-0.4.jar
   ```

2. Start the Spark shell and provide the `spark-streaming-kafka` library:

   ```
   $ spark-shell --jars spark-streaming-kafka_2.10-1.2.0.jar,
   kafka_2.10-0.8.1.jar,metrics-core-2.2.0.jar,zkclient-0.4.jar
   ```

3. Stream specific imports:

   ```
   scala> import org.apache.spark.streaming.{Seconds,
   StreamingContext}
   ```

4. Import for implicit conversion:

```
scala> import org.apache.spark._
scala> import org.apache.spark.streaming._
scala> import org.apache.spark.streaming.StreamingContext._
scala> import org.apache.spark.streaming.kafka.KafkaUtils
```

5. Create `StreamingContext` with a 2 second batch interval:

```
scala> val ssc = new StreamingContext(sc, Seconds(2))
```

6. Set Kafka-specific variables:

```
scala> val zkQuorum = "localhost:2181"
scala> val group = "test-group"
scala> val topics = "test"
scala> val numThreads = 1
```

7. Create `topicMap`:

```
scala> val topicMap = topics.split(",").map((_,numThreads.toInt)).
toMap
```

8. Create Kafka DStream:

```
scala> val lineMap = KafkaUtils.createStream(ssc, zkQuorum, group,
topicMap)
```

9. Pull the value out of lineMap:

```
scala> val lines = lineMap.map(_._2)
```

10. Create `flatMap` of values:

```
scala> val words = lines.flatMap(_.split(" "))
```

11. Create the key-value pair of (word,occurrence):

```
scala> val pair = words.map( x => (x,1))
```

12. Do the word count for a sliding window:

```
scala> val wordCounts = pair.reduceByKeyAndWindow(_ + _, _ - _,
Minutes(10), Seconds(2), 2)
scala> wordCounts.print
```

13. Set the `checkpoint` directory:

```
scala> ssc.checkpoint("hdfs://localhost:9000/user/hduser/
checkpoint")
```

14. Start `StreamingContext`:

```
scala> ssc.start
scala> ssc.awaitTermination
```

15. Publish a message on the `test` topic in Kafka in another window:

```
$ /opt/infoobjects/kafka/bin/kafka-console-producer.sh --broker-
list localhost:9092 --topic test
```

16. Now, publish messages on Kafka by pressing *Enter* at step 15 and after every message.
17. Now, as you publish messages on Kafka, you will see them in the Spark shell:

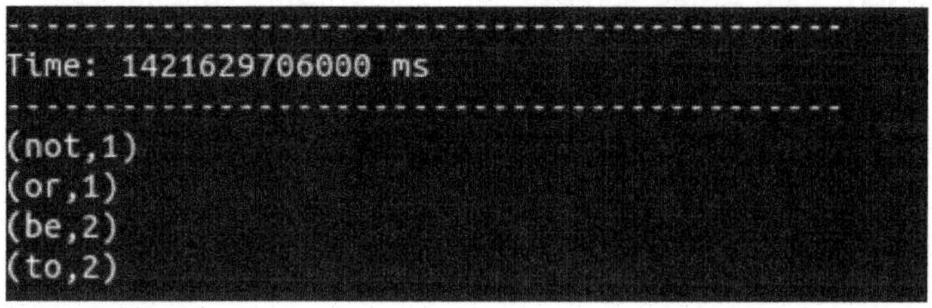

There's more...

Let's say you want to maintain a running count of the occurrence of each word. Spark Streaming has a feature for this called `updateStateByKey` operation. The `updateStateByKey` operation allows you to maintain any arbitrary state while updating it with the new information supplied.

This arbitrary state can be an aggregation value, or just a change in state (like the mood of a user on twitter). Perform the following steps:

1. Let's call `updateStateByKey` on pairs RDD:

```
scala> val runningCounts = wordCounts.updateStateByKey( (values:
Seq[Int], state: Option[Int]) => Some(state.sum + values.sum))
```

> The `updateStateByKey` operation returns a new "state" DStream where the state for each key is updated by applying the given function on the previous state of the key and the new values for the key. This can be used to maintain arbitrary state data for each key.
>
> There are two steps involved in making this operation work:
>
> - Define the state
> - Define the state `update` function
>
> The `updateStateByKey` operation is called once for each key, values represent the sequence of values associated with that key, very much like MapReduce and the state can be any arbitrary state, which we chose to make `Option[Int]`. With every call in step 18, the previous state gets updated by adding the sum of current values to it.

2. Print the results:

```
scala> runningCounts.print
```

3. The following are all the steps combined to maintain the arbitrary state using the `updateStateByKey` operation:

```
Scala> :paste
import org.apache.spark.streaming.{Seconds, StreamingContext}
 import org.apache.spark._
 import org.apache.spark.streaming._
 import org.apache.spark.streaming.kafka._
 import org.apache.spark.streaming.StreamingContext._
 val ssc = new StreamingContext(sc, Seconds(2))
 val zkQuorum = "localhost:2181"
 val group = "test-group"
 val topics = "test"
 val numThreads = 1
 val topicMap = topics.split(",").map((_,numThreads.toInt)).toMap
 val lineMap = KafkaUtils.createStream(ssc, zkQuorum, group,
topicMap)
 val lines = lineMap.map(_._2)
 val words = lines.flatMap(_.split(" "))
 val pairs = words.map(x => (x,1))
 val runningCounts = pairs.updateStateByKey( (values: Seq[Int],
state: Option[Int]) => Some(state.sum + values.sum))
 runningCounts.print
ssc.checkpoint("hdfs://localhost:9000/user/hduser/checkpoint")
 ssc.start
 ssc.awaitTermination
```

4. Run it by pressing *Ctrl* + *D* (which executes the code pasted using `:paste`).

6
Getting Started with Machine Learning Using MLlib

This chapter is divided into the following recipes:

- Creating vectors
- Creating a labeled point
- Creating matrices
- Calculating summary statistics
- Calculating correlation
- Doing hypothesis testing
- Creating machine learning pipelines using ML

Introduction

The following is Wikipedia's definition of machine learning:

> *"Machine learning is a scientific discipline that explores the construction and study of algorithms that can learn from data."*

Essentially, machine learning is making use of past data to make predictions about the future. Machine learning heavily depends upon statistical analysis and methodology.

In statistics, there are four types of measurement scales:

Scale type	Description
Nominal Scale	=, ≠ Identifies categories Can't be numeric Example: male, female
Ordinal Scale	=, ≠, <, > Nominal scale + Ranks from least important to most important Example: corporate hierarchy
Interval Scale	=, ≠, <, >, +, - Ordinal scale + distance between observations Numbers assigned to observations indicate order Difference between any consecutive values is same as others 60° temperature is not the double of 30°
Ratio Scale	=, ≠, <, >, +, ×, ÷ Interval scale +ratios of observations $20 is twice as costly as $10

Another distinction that can be made among the data is between the continuous and discrete data. Continuous data can take any value. Most data belonging to the interval and ratio scale is continuous.

Discrete variables can take on only particular values and there are clear boundaries between the values. For example, a house can have two or three rooms but not 2.75 rooms. Data belonging to nominal and ordinal scale is always discrete.

MLlib is the Spark's library for machine learning. In this chapter, we will focus on the fundamentals of machine learning.

Creating vectors

Before understanding Vectors, let's focus on what is a point. A point is just a set of numbers. This set of numbers or coordinates defines the point's position in space. The numbers of coordinates determine dimensions of the space.

We can visualize space with up to three dimensions. Space with more than three dimensions is called **hyperspace**. Let's put this spatial metaphor to use.

Let's start with a person. A person has the following dimensions:

- Weight
- Height
- Age

We are working in three-dimensional space here. Thus, the interpretation of point (160,69,24) would be 160 lb weight, 69 inches height, and 24 years age.

> Points and vectors are same thing. Dimensions in vectors are called **features**. In another way, we can define a feature as an individual measurable property of a phenomenon being observed.

Spark has local vectors and matrices and also distributed matrices. Distributed matrix is backed by one or more RDDs. A local vector has numeric indices and double values, and is stored on a single machine.

There are two types of local vectors in MLlib: dense and sparse. A dense vector is backed by an array of its values, while a sparse vector is backed by two parallel arrays, one for indices and another for values.

So, person data (160,69,24) will be represented as [160.0,69.0,24.0] using dense vector and as (3,[0,1,2],[160.0,69.0,24.0]) using sparse vector format.

Whether to make a vector sparse or dense depends upon how many null values or 0s it has. Let's take a case of a vector with 10,000 values with 9,000 of them being 0. If we use dense vector format, it would be a simple structure, but 90 percent of space would be wasted. Sparse vector format would work out better here as it would only keep indices, which are non-zero.

Sparse data is very common and Spark supports the `libsvm` format for it which stores one feature vector per line.

How to do it...

1. Start the Spark shell:

   ```
   $ spark-shell
   ```

2. Import the MLlib vector explicitly (not to confuse with other vector classes):

   ```
   Scala> import org.apache.spark.mllib.linalg.{Vectors,Vector}
   ```

3. Create a dense vector:

   ```
   scala> val dvPerson = Vectors.dense(160.0,69.0,24.0)
   ```

4. Create a sparse vector:

```
scala> val svPerson = Vectors.sparse(3,Array(0,1,2),Arr
ay(160.0,69.0,24.0))
```

How it works...

The following is the method signature of `vectors.dense`:

```
def dense(values: Array[Double]): Vector
```

Here, values represent double array of elements in the vector.

The following is the method signature of `Vectors.sparse`:

```
def sparse(size: Int, indices: Array[Int], values: Array[Double]):
Vector
```

Here, `size` represents the size of the vector, `indices` is an array of indices, and `values` is an array of values as doubles. Do make sure you specify `double` as datatype or use decimal in at least one value; otherwise it will throw an exception for the dataset, which has only integer.

Creating a labeled point

Labeled point is a local vector (sparse/dense), which has an associated label with it. Labeled data is used in supervised learning to help train algorithms. You will get to know more about it in the next chapter.

Label is stored as a double value in `LabeledPoint`. It means that when you have categorical labels, they need to be mapped to double values. What value you assign to a category is immaterial and is only a matter of convenience.

Type	Label values
Binary classification	0 or 1
Multiclass classification	0, 1, 2...
Regression	Decimal values

How to do it...

1. Start the Spark shell:

```
$spark-shell
```

2. Import the MLlib vector explicitly:

```
scala> import org.apache.spark.mllib.linalg.{Vectors,Vector}
```

3. Import the `LabeledPoint`:

   ```
   scala> import org.apache.spark.mllib.regression.LabeledPoint
   ```

4. Create a labeled point with a positive label and dense vector:

   ```
   scala> val willBuySUV = LabeledPoint(1.0,Vectors.
   dense(300.0,80,40))
   ```

5. Create a labeled point with a negative label and dense vector:

   ```
   scala> val willNotBuySUV = LabeledPoint(0.0,Vectors.
   dense(150.0,60,25))
   ```

6. Create a labeled point with a positive label and sparse vector:

   ```
   scala> val willBuySUV = LabeledPoint(1.0,Vectors.sparse(3,Array(0,
   1,2),Array(300.0,80,40)))
   ```

7. Create a labeled point with a negative label and sparse vector:

   ```
   scala> val willNotBuySUV = LabeledPoint(0.0,Vectors.sparse(3,Array
   (0,1,2),Array(150.0,60,25)))
   ```

8. Create a `libsvm` file with the same data:

   ```
   $vi person_libsvm.txt (libsvm indices start with 1)
   0  1:150 2:60 3:25
   1  1:300 2:80 3:40
   ```

9. Upload `person_libsvm.txt` to `hdfs`:

   ```
   $ hdfs dfs -put person_libsvm.txt person_libsvm.txt
   ```

10. Do a few more imports:

    ```
    scala> import org.apache.spark.mllib.util.MLUtils
    scala> import org.apache.spark.rdd.RDD
    ```

11. Load data from `libsvm` file:

    ```
    scala> val persons = MLUtils.loadLibSVMFile(sc,"person_libsvm.
    txt")
    ```

Creating matrices

Matrix is simply a table to represent multiple feature vectors. A matrix that can be stored on one machine is called **local matrix** and the one that can be distributed across the cluster is called **distributed matrix**.

Local matrices have integer-based indices, while distributed matrices have long-based indices. Both have values as doubles.

There are three types of distributed matrices:

- `RowMatrix`: This has each row as a feature vector.
- `IndexedRowMatrix`: This also has row indices.
- `CoordinateMatrix`: This is simply a matrix of `MatrixEntry`. A `MatrixEntry` represents an entry in the matrix represented by its row and column index.

How to do it...

1. Start the Spark shell:

```
$spark-shell
```

2. Import the matrix-related classes:

```
scala> import org.apache.spark.mllib.linalg.{Vectors,Matrix,
Matrices}
```

3. Create a dense local matrix:

```
scala> val people = Matrices.dense(3,2,Array(150d,60d,25d,
300d,80d,40d))
```

4. Create a `personRDD` as RDD of vectors:

```
scala> val personRDD = sc.parallelize(List(Vectors.
dense(150,60,25), Vectors.dense(300,80,40)))
```

5. Import `RowMatrix` and related classes:

```
scala> import org.apache.spark.mllib.linalg.distributed.
{IndexedRow, IndexedRowMatrix,RowMatrix, CoordinateMatrix,
MatrixEntry}
```

6. Create a row matrix of `personRDD`:

```
scala> val personMat = new RowMatrix(personRDD)
```

7. Print the number of rows:

```
scala> print(personMat.numRows)
```

8. Print the number of columns:

```
scala> print(personMat.numCols)
```

9. Create an RDD of indexed rows:

```
scala> val personRDD = sc.parallelize(List(IndexedRow(0L, Vectors.
dense(150,60,25)), IndexedRow(1L, Vectors.dense(300,80,40))))
```

10. Create an indexed row matrix:

```
scala> val pirmat = new IndexedRowMatrix(personRDD)
```

11. Print the number of rows:

```
scala> print(pirmat.numRows)
```

12. Print the number of columns:

```
scala> print(pirmat.numCols)
```

13. Convert the indexed row matrix back to row matrix:

```
scala> val personMat = pirmat.toRowMatrix
```

14. Create an RDD of matrix entries:

```
scala> val meRDD = sc.parallelize(List(
  MatrixEntry(0,0,150),
  MatrixEntry(1,0,60),
MatrixEntry(2,0,25),
MatrixEntry(0,1,300),
MatrixEntry(1,1,80),
MatrixEntry(2,1,40)
))
```

15. Create a coordinate matrix:

```
scala> val pcmat = new CoordinateMatrix(meRDD)
```

16. Print the number of rows:

```
scala> print(pcmat.numRows)
```

17. Print the number of columns:

```
scala> print(pcmat.numCols)
```

Calculating summary statistics

Summary statistics is used to summarize observations to get a collective sense of the data. The summary includes the following:

- Central tendency of data—mean, mode, median
- Spread of data—variance, standard deviation
- Boundary conditions—min, max

This recipe covers how to produce summary statistics.

How to do it...

1. Start the Spark shell:

```
$ spark-shell
```

2. Import the matrix-related classes:

```
scala> import org.apache.spark.mllib.linalg.{Vectors,Vector}
scala> import org.apache.spark.mllib.stat.Statistics
```

3. Create a `personRDD` as RDD of vectors:

```
scala> val personRDD = sc.parallelize(List(Vectors.
dense(150,60,25), Vectors.dense(300,80,40)))
```

4. Compute the column summary statistics:

```
scala> val summary = Statistics.colStats(personRDD)
```

5. Print the mean of this summary:

```
scala> print(summary.mean)
```

6. Print the variance:

```
scala> print(summary.variance)
```

7. Print the non-zero values in each column:

```
scala> print(summary.numNonzeros)
```

8. Print the sample size:

```
scala> print(summary.count)
```

9. Print the max value of each column:

```
scala> print(summary.max)
```

Calculating correlation

Correlation is a statistical relationship between two variables such that when one variable changes, it leads to a change in the other variable. Correlation analysis measures the extent to which the two variables are correlated.

If an increase in one variable leads to an increase in another, it is called a **positive correlation**. If an increase in one variable leads to a decrease in the other, it is a **negative correlation**.

Spark supports two correlation algorithms: Pearson and Spearman. Pearson algorithm works with two continuous variables, such as a person's height and weight or house size and house price. Spearman deals with one continuous and one categorical variable, for example, zip code and house price.

Getting ready

Let's use some real data so that we can calculate correlation more meaningfully. The following are the size and price of houses in the City of Saratoga, California, in early 2014:

House size (sq ft)	Price
2100	$1,620,000
2300	$1,690,000
2046	$1,400,000
4314	$2,000,000
1244	$1,060,000
4608	$3,830,000
2173	$1,230,000
2750	$2,400,000
4010	$3,380,000
1959	$1,480,000

How to do it...

1. Start the Spark shell:

   ```
   $ spark-shell
   ```

2. Import the statistics and related classes:

   ```
   scala> import org.apache.spark.mllib.linalg._
   scala> import org.apache.spark.mllib.stat.Statistics
   ```

3. Create an RDD of house sizes:

   ```
   scala> val sizes = sc.parallelize(List(2100, 2300, 2046, 4314,
   1244, 4608, 2173, 2750, 4010, 1959.0))
   ```

4. Create an RDD of house prices:

   ```
   scala> val prices = sc.parallelize(List(1620000 , 1690000,
   1400000, 2000000, 1060000, 3830000, 1230000, 2400000, 3380000,
   1480000.00))
   ```

5. Compute the correlation:

   ```
   scala> val correlation = Statistics.corr(sizes,prices)
   correlation: Double = 0.8577177736252577
   ```

   `0.85` means a very strong positive correlation.

Since we do not have a specific algorithm here, it is, by default, Pearson. The `corr` method is overloaded to take the algorithm name as the third parameter.

6. Compute the correlation with Pearson:

```
scala> val correlation = Statistics.corr(sizes,prices)
```

7. Compute the correlation with Spearman:

```
scala> val correlation = Statistics.corr(sizes,prices,"spearman")
```

Both the variables in the preceding example are continuous, so Spearman assumes the size to be discrete. A better example of Spearman's use would be zip code versus price.

Doing hypothesis testing

Hypothesis testing is a way of determining probability that a given hypothesis is true. Let's say a sample data suggests that females tend to vote more for the Democratic Party. This may or may not be true for the larger population. What if this pattern is there in the sample data just by chance?

Another way to look at the goal of hypothesis testing is to answer this question: If a sample has a pattern in it, what are the chances of the pattern being there just by chance?

How do we do it? There is a saying that the best way to prove something is to try to disprove it.

The hypothesis to disprove is called **null hypothesis**. Hypothesis testing works with categorical data. Let's look at the example of a gallop poll of party affiliations.

Party	Male	Female
Democratic Party	32	41
Republican Party	28	25
Independent	34	26

How to do it...

1. Start the Spark shell:

```
$ spark-shell
```

2. Import the relevant classes:

```
scala> import org.apache.spark.mllib.stat.Statistics
scala> import org.apache.spark.mllib.linalg.{Vector,Vectors}
scala> import org.apache.spark.mllib.linalg.{Matrix, Matrices}
```

3. Create a vector for the Democratic Party:

```
scala> val dems = Vectors.dense(32.0,41.0)
```

4. Create a vector for the Republican Party:

```
scala> val reps= Vectors.dense(28.0,25.0)
```

5. Create a vector for the Independents:

```
scala> val indies = Vectors.dense(34.0,26.0)
```

6. Do the chi-square goodness of fit test of the observed data against uniform distribution:

```
scala> val dfit = Statistics.chiSqTest(dems)
scala> val rfit = Statistics.chiSqTest(reps)
scala> val ifit = Statistics.chiSqTest(indies)
```

7. Print the goodness of fit results:

```
scala> print(dfit)
scala> print(rfit)
scala> print(ifit)
```

8. Create the input matrix:

```
scala> val mat = Matrices.dense(2,3,Array(32.0,41.0, 28.0,25.0,
34.0,26.0))
```

9. Do the chi-square independence test:

```
scala> val in = Statistics.chiSqTest(mat)
```

10. Print the independence test results:

```
scala> print(in)
```

Creating machine learning pipelines using ML

Spark ML is a new library in Spark to build machine learning pipelines. This library is being developed along with MLlib. It helps to combine multiple machine learning algorithms into a single pipeline, and uses DataFrame as dataset.

Getting ready

Let's first understand some of the basic concepts in Spark ML. It uses transformers to transform one DataFrame into another DataFrame. One example of simple transformations can be to append a column. You can think of it as being equivalent to "alter table" in relational world.

Estimator, on the other hand, represents a machine learning algorithm, which learns from the data. Input to an estimator is a DataFrame and output is a transformer. Every Estimator has a `fit()` method, which does the job of training the algorithm.

A machine learning pipeline is defined as a sequence of stages; each stage can be either an estimator or a transformer.

The example we are going to use in this recipe is whether someone is a basketball player or not a basketball player. For this, we are going to have a pipeline of one estimator and one transformer.

Estimator gets training data to train the algorithms and then transformer makes predictions.

For now, assume `LogisticRegression` to be the machine learning algorithm we are using. We will explain the details about `LogisticRegression` along with other algorithms in the subsequent chapters.

How to do it...

1. Start the Spark shell:

   ```
   $ spark-shell
   ```

2. Do the imports:

   ```
   scala> import org.apache.spark.mllib.linalg.{Vector,Vectors}
   scala> import org.apache.spark.mllib.regression.LabeledPoint
   scala> import org.apache.spark.ml.classification.
   LogisticRegression
   ```

3. Create a labeled point for Lebron who is a basketball player, is 80 inches tall height and weighs 250 lbs:

   ```
   scala> val lebron = LabeledPoint(1.0,Vectors.dense(80.0,250.0))
   ```

4. Create a labeled point for Tim who is not a basketball player, is 70 inches tall height and weighs 150 lbs:

   ```
   scala> val tim = LabeledPoint(0.0,Vectors.dense(70.0,150.0))
   ```

5. Create a labeled point for Brittany who is a basketball player, is 80 inches tall height and weighs 207 lbs:

```
scala> val brittany = LabeledPoint(1.0,Vectors.dense(80.0,207.0))
```

6. Create a labeled point for Stacey who is not a basketball player, is 65 inches tall, and weighs 120 lbs:

```
scala> val stacey = LabeledPoint(0.0,Vectors.dense(65.0,120.0))
```

7. Create a training RDD:

```
scala> val trainingRDD = sc.parallelize(List(lebron,tim,brittany,s
tacey))
```

8. Create a training DataFrame:

```
scala> val trainingDF = trainingRDD.toDF
```

9. Create a `LogisticRegression` estimator:

```
scala> val estimator = new LogisticRegression
```

10. Create a transformer by fitting the estimator with training DataFrame:

```
scala> val transformer = estimator.fit(trainingDF)
```

11. Now, let's create a test data—John is 90 inches tall and weighs 270 lbs, and is a basketball player:

```
scala> val john = Vectors.dense(90.0,270.0)
```

12. Create another test data—Tom is 62 inches tall and weighs 150 lbs, and is not a basketball player:

```
scala> val tom = Vectors.dense(62.0,120.0)
```

13. Create a training RDD:

```
scala> val testRDD = sc.parallelize(List(john,tom))
```

14. Create a `Features` case class:

```
scala> case class Feature(v:Vector)
```

15. Map the `testRDD` to an RDD for `Features`:

```
scala> val featuresRDD = testRDD.map( v => Feature(v))
```

16. Convert `featuresRDD` into a DataFrame with column name `"features"`:

```
scala> val featuresDF = featuresRDD.toDF("features")
```

17. Transform `featuresDF` by adding the `predictions` column to it:

```
scala> val predictionsDF = transformer.transform(featuresDF)
```

18. Print the `predictionsDF`:

```
scala> predictionsDF.foreach(println)
```

19. `PredictionDF`, as you can see, creates three columns—`rawPrediction`, `probability`, and `prediction`—besides keeping features. Let's select only `features` and `prediction`:

```
scala> val shorterPredictionsDF = predictionsDF.
select("features","prediction")
```

20. Rename the prediction to `isBasketBallPlayer`:

```
scala> val playerDF = shorterPredictionsDF.toDF("features","isBask
etBallPlayer")
```

21. Print the schema for `playerDF`:

```
scala> playerDF.printSchema
```

7

Supervised Learning with MLlib – Regression

This chapter is divided into the following recipes:

- Using linear regression
- Understanding the cost function
- Doing linear regression with lasso
- Doing ridge regression

Introduction

The following is Wikipedia's definition of supervised learning:

> *"Supervised learning is the machine learning task of inferring a function from labeled training data."*

Supervised learning has two steps:

- Train the algorithm with training dataset; it is like giving questions and their answers first
- Use test dataset to ask another set of questions to the trained algorithm

There are two types of supervised learning algorithms:

- **Regression**: This predicts continuous value output, such as house price.
- **Classification**: This predicts discreet valued output (0 or 1) called label, such as whether an e-mail is a spam or not. Classification is not limited to two values; it can have multiple values such as marking an e-mail important, not important, urgent, and so on (0, 1, 2...).

[We are going to cover regression in this chapter and classification in the next.]

As an example dataset for regression, we will use the recently sold house data of the City of Saratoga, CA, as a training set to train the algorithm. Once the algorithm is trained, we will ask it to predict the house price by the given size of that house. The following figure illustrates the workflow:

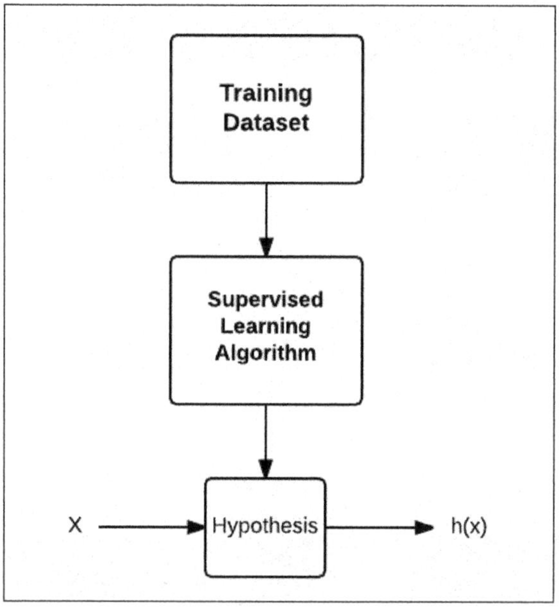

Hypothesis, for what it does, may sound like a misnomer here, and you may think that prediction function may be a better name, but the word hypothesis is used for historic reasons.

If we use only one feature to predict the outcome, it is called **bivariate analysis**. When we have multiple features, it is called **multivariate analysis**. In fact, we can have as many features as we like. One such algorithm, **support vector machines** (**SVM**), which we will cover in the next chapter, in fact, allows you to have an infinite number of features.

This chapter will cover how we can do supervised learning using MLlib, Spark's machine learning library.

[Mathematical explanations have been provided in as simple a way as possible, but you can feel free to skip math and directly go to *How to do it...* section.]

Using linear regression

Linear regression is the approach to model the value of a response variable *y*, based on one or more predictor variables or feature *x*.

Getting ready

Let's use some housing data to predict the price of a house based on its size. The following are the sizes and prices of houses in the City of Saratoga, CA, in early 2014:

House size (sq ft)	Price
2100	$ 1,620,000
2300	$ 1,690,000
2046	$ 1,400,000
4314	$ 2,000,000
1244	$ 1,060,000
4608	$ 3,830,000
2173	$ 1,230,000
2750	$ 2,400,000
4010	$ 3,380,000
1959	$ 1,480,000

Here's a graphical representation of the same:

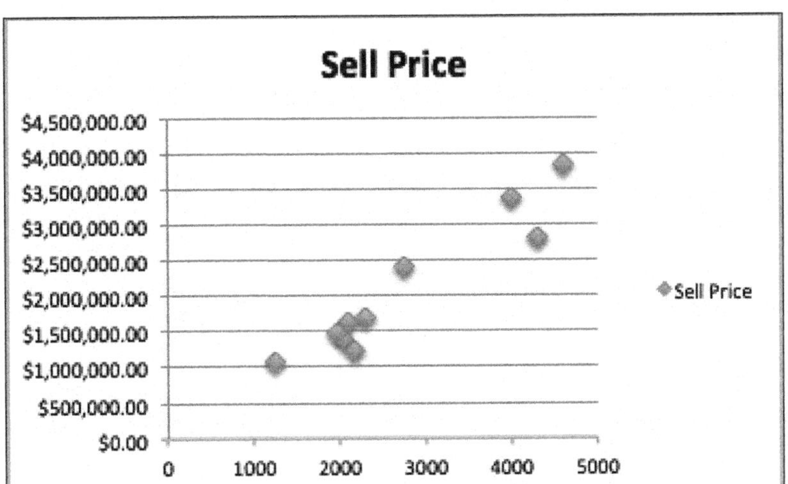

How to do it...

1. Start the Spark shell:

   ```
   $ spark-shell
   ```

2. Import the statistics and related classes:

   ```
   scala> import org.apache.spark.mllib.linalg.Vectors
   scala> import org.apache.spark.mllib.regression.LabeledPoint
   scala> import org.apache.spark.mllib.regression.
   LinearRegressionWithSGD
   ```

3. Create the `LabeledPoint` array with the house price as the label:

   ```
   scala> val points = Array(
   LabeledPoint(1620000,Vectors.dense(2100)),
   LabeledPoint(1690000,Vectors.dense(2300)),
   LabeledPoint(1400000,Vectors.dense(2046)),
   LabeledPoint(2000000,Vectors.dense(4314)),
   LabeledPoint(1060000,Vectors.dense(1244)),
   LabeledPoint(3830000,Vectors.dense(4608)),
   LabeledPoint(1230000,Vectors.dense(2173)),
   LabeledPoint(2400000,Vectors.dense(2750)),
   LabeledPoint(3380000,Vectors.dense(4010)),
   LabeledPoint(1480000,Vectors.dense(1959))
   )
   ```

4. Create an RDD of the preceding data:

   ```
   scala> val pricesRDD = sc.parallelize(points)
   ```

5. Train a model using this data using 100 iterations. Here, step size has been kept small to account for very large values of response variables, that is, the house price. The fourth parameter is a fraction of the dataset to use per iteration, and the last parameter is the initial set of weights to be used (weights of different features):

   ```
   scala> val model = LinearRegressionWithSGD.train(pricesRDD,100,0.0
   000006,1.0,Vectors.zeros(1))
   ```

6. Predict the price for a house with 2,500 sq ft:

   ```
   scala> val prediction = model.predict(Vectors.dense(2500))
   ```

House size is just one predictor variable. House price depends upon other variables, such as lot size, age of the house, and so on. The more variables you have, the better your prediction will be.

Understanding cost function

Cost function or loss function is a very important function in machine learning algorithms. Most algorithms have some form of cost function and the goal is to minimize that. Parameters, which affect cost function, such as `stepSize` in the last recipe, need to be set by hand. Therefore, understanding the whole concept of cost function is very important.

In this recipe, we are going to analyze cost function for linear regression. Linear regression is a simple algorithm to understand and it will help readers understand the role of cost functions for even complex algorithms.

Let's go back to linear regression. The goal is to find the best-fitting line so that the mean square of error is minimum. Here, we are referring error as the difference between the value as per the best-fitting line and the actual value of the response variable for the training dataset.

For a simple case of single predicate variable, the best-fit line can be written as:

$$y = \theta_0 + \theta_1 x$$

This function is also called **hypothesis function**, and can be written as:

$$h(x) = \theta_0 + \theta_1 x$$

The goal of the linear regression is to find the best-fit line. On this line, θ_0 represents intercept on the *y* axis and θ_1 represents the slope of the line as obvious from the following equation:

$$h(x) = \theta_0 + \theta_1 x$$

We have to choose θ_0 and θ_1 in a way that *h(x)* is closest to *y* for the training dataset. So, for the ith data point, the square of distance between the line and data point is:

$$\left(x^i - x^i\right)^2 + \left(h\left(x^i\right) - y^i\right)^2$$
$$= \left(h\left(x^i\right) - y^i\right)^2$$

To put it in words, this is the square of the difference between the predicted house price and the actual price the house got sold for. Now, let's take average of this value across the training dataset:

$$\frac{1}{2m}\sum_{i=1}^{m}\left(h(x)^{i}-y^{i}\right)^{2}$$

The preceding equation is called the cost function *J* for linear regression. The goal is to minimize this cost function.

$$J(\theta_0,\theta_1)=\frac{1}{2m}\sum_{i=1}^{m}\left(h(x)^{i}-y^{i}\right)^{2}$$

This cost function is also called **squared error function**. Both θ_0 and theta θ_1 follow convex curve independently if they are plotted against *J*.

Let's take a very simple example of dataset of three values, (1,1), (2,2), and (3,3), to make the calculation easy:

$$\left(x^{1},y^{1}\right)=(1,1)$$
$$\left(x^{2},y^{2}\right)=(2,2)$$
$$\left(x^{3},y^{3}\right)=(3,3)$$

Let's assume θ_1 is 0, that is, the best-fit line parallel to the *x* axis. In the first case, assume that the best-fit line is the *x* axis, that is, *y=0*. The following will be the value of the cost function:

$$(\theta_0,\theta_1)=(0,0)$$
$$J(\theta_0)=\frac{1}{2\times 3}\sum_{i=1}^{3}\left(y^{i}\right)^{2}$$
$$=\frac{1}{2\times 3}(1+4+9)=\frac{14}{6}=2.33$$

Now, let's move this line slightly up to *y=1*. The following will be the value of the cost function:

$$(\theta_0, \theta_1) = (1,0)$$
$$J(\theta_0) = \frac{1}{2\times 3}\sum_{i=1}^{3}\left(1-y^i\right)^2$$
$$= \frac{1}{2\times 3}(0+1+4) = \frac{5}{6} = 0.83$$

Now, let's move this line further up to *y=2*. Then, the following will be the value of the cost function:

$$(\theta_0, \theta_1) = (2,0)$$
$$J(\theta_0) = \frac{1}{2\times 3}\sum_{i=1}^{3}\left(2-y^i\right)^2$$
$$= \frac{1}{2\times 3}(1+0+1) = \frac{2}{6} = 0.33$$

Now, when we move this line further up to *y=3*, the following will be the value of the cost function:

$$(\theta_0, \theta_1) = (3,0)$$
$$J(\theta_0) = \frac{1}{2\times 3}\sum_{i=1}^{3}\left(3-y^i\right)^2$$
$$= \frac{1}{2\times 3}(4+1+0) = \frac{5}{6} = 0.83$$

Now, let's move this line further up to *y=4*. The following will be the value of the cost function:

$$(\theta_0, \theta_1) = (4,0)$$
$$J(\theta_0) = \frac{1}{2\times 3}\sum_{i=1}^{3}\left(4-y^i\right)^2$$
$$= \frac{1}{2\times 3}(9+4+1) = \frac{14}{6} = 2.33$$

So, you saw that the cost function value first decreased, and then increased again like this:

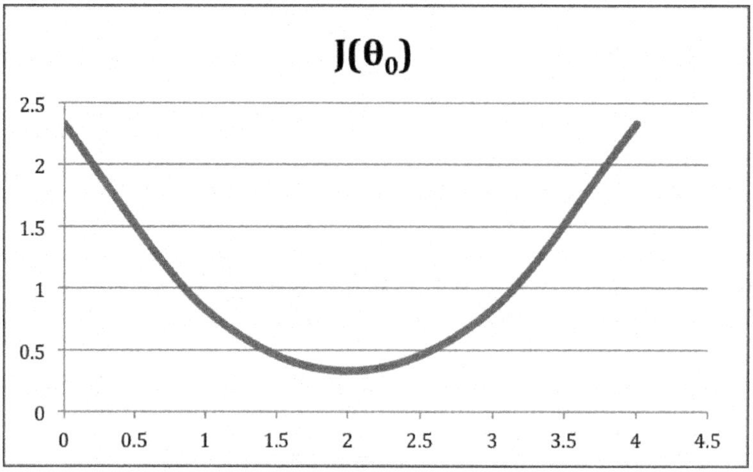

Now, let's repeat the exercise by making θ_0 0 and using different values of θ_1.

In the first case, assume the best-fit line is the *x* axis, that is, *y=0*. The following will be the value of the cost function:

$$(\theta_0, \theta_1) = (0, 0)$$

$$J(\theta_1) = \frac{1}{2 \times 3} \sum_{i=1}^{3} \left(y^i\right)^2$$

$$= \frac{1}{2 \times 3}(1 + 4 + 9) = \frac{14}{6} = 2.33$$

Now, let's use a slope of 0.5. The following will be the value of the cost function:

$$(\theta_0, \theta_1) = (0, 0.5)$$

$$J(\theta_1) = \frac{1}{2 \times 3} \sum_{i=1}^{3} \left(0.5x^i - y^i\right)^2$$

$$= \frac{1}{2 \times 3}(0.25 + 0 + 2.25) = \frac{2.5}{6} = 0.41$$

Now, let's use a slope of 1. The following will be the value of the cost function:

$$(\theta_0, \theta_1) = (0, 1)$$

$$J(\theta_1) = \frac{1}{2 \times 3} \sum_{i=1}^{3} \left(x^i - y^i \right)^2$$

$$= \frac{1}{2 \times 3} (0 + 0 + 0) = 0$$

Now, when we use a slope of 1.5, the following will be the value of the cost function:

$$(\theta_0, \theta_1) = (0, 1.5)$$

$$J(\theta_1) = \frac{1}{2 \times 3} \sum_{i=1}^{3} \left(1.5x^i - y^i \right)^2$$

$$= \frac{1}{2 \times 3} (0.25 + 1 + 2.25) = \frac{3.5}{6} = 0.58$$

Now, let's use a slope of 2.0. The following will be the value of the cost function:

$$(\theta_0, \theta_1) = (0, 2.0)$$

$$J(\theta_1) = \frac{1}{2 \times 3} \sum_{i=1}^{3} \left(2x^i - y^i \right)^2$$

$$= \frac{1}{2 \times 3} (1 + 4 + 9) = \frac{14}{6} = 2.33$$

As you can see in both the graphs, the minimum value of *J* is when slope or gradient of curve is 0.

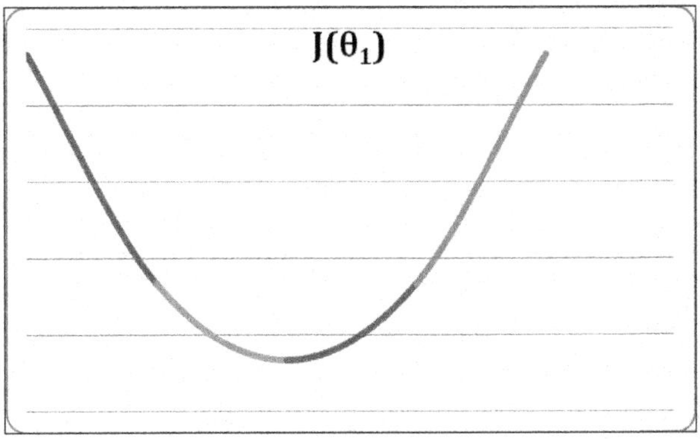

When both θ_0 and θ_1 are mapped to a 3D space, it becomes like the shape of a bowl with the minimum value of the cost function being at the bottom of it.

This approach to arrive at this minimum is called **gradient descent**. In Spark, the implementation is stochastic gradient descent.

Doing linear regression with lasso

The lasso is a shrinkage and selection method for linear regression. It minimizes the usual sum of squared errors, with a bound on the sum of the absolute values of the coefficients. It is based on the original lasso paper found at `http://statweb.stanford.edu/~tibs/lasso/lasso.pdf`.

The least square method we used in the last recipe is also called **ordinary least squares** (**OLS**). OLS has two challenges:

- **Prediction accuracy**: Predictions made using OLS usually have low forecast bias and high variance. Prediction accuracy can be improved by shrinking some coefficients (or even making them zero). There will be some increase in bias, but overall prediction accuracy will improve.
- **Interpretation**: With a large number of predictors, it is desirable to find a subset of them that exhibits the strongest effect (correlation).

> Bias versus variance
>
> There are two primary reasons behind prediction error: bias and variance. The best way to understand bias and variance is to look at a case where we are doing predictions on the same dataset multiple times.
>
> Bias is an estimate of how far the predicted results are from the actual values, and variance is an estimate of the difference in predicted values among different predictions.
>
> Generally, adding more features helps to reduce bias, as can easily be understood. If, in building a prediction model, we have left out some features with significant correlation, it would lead to significant error.
>
> If your model has high variance, you can remove features to reduce it. A bigger dataset also helps to reduce variance.

Here, we are going to use a simple dataset, which is ill-posed. An ill-posed dataset is a dataset where the sample data size is smaller than the number of predictors.

y	x0	x1	x2	x3	x4	x5	x6	x7	x8
1	5	3	1	2	1	3	2	2	1
2	9	8	8	9	7	9	8	7	9

You can easily guess that, here, out of nine predictors, only two have a strong correlation with *y*, that is, *x0* and *x1*. We will use this dataset with the lasso algorithm to see its validity.

How to do it...

1. Start the Spark shell:

   ```
   $ spark-shell
   ```

2. Import the statistics and related classes:

   ```
   scala> import org.apache.spark.mllib.linalg.Vectors
   scala> import org.apache.spark.mllib.regression.LabeledPoint
   scala> import org.apache.spark.mllib.regression.LassoWithSGD
   ```

3. Create the `LabeledPoint` array with the house price as the label:

   ```
   scala> val points = Array(
   LabeledPoint(1,Vectors.dense(5,3,1,2,1,3,2,2,1)),
   LabeledPoint(2,Vectors.dense(9,8,8,9,7,9,8,7,9))
   )
   ```

4. Create an RDD of the preceding data:

   ```
   scala> val rdd = sc.parallelize(points)
   ```

5. Train a model using this data using 100 iterations. Here, the step size and regularization parameter have been set by hand:

   ```
   scala> val model = LassoWithSGD.train(rdd,100,0.02,2.0)
   ```

6. Check how many predictors have their coefficients set to zero:

   ```
   scala> model.weights
   org.apache.spark.mllib.linalg.Vector = [0.13455106581619633,0.0224
   0732644670294,0.0,0.0,0.0,0.01360995990267153,0.0,0.0,0.0]
   ```

As you can see, six out of nine predictors have got their coefficients set to zero. This is the primary feature of lasso: any predictor it thinks is not useful, it literally moves them out of equation by setting their coefficients to zero.

Doing ridge regression

An alternate way to lasso to improve prediction quality is ridge regression. While in lasso, a lot of features get their coefficients set to zero and, therefore, eliminated from an equation, in ridge, predictors or features are penalized, but are never set to zero.

How to do it...

1. Start the Spark shell:

```
$ spark-shell
```

2. Import the statistics and related classes:

```
scala> import org.apache.spark.mllib.linalg.Vectors
scala> import org.apache.spark.mllib.regression.LabeledPoint
scala> import org.apache.spark.mllib.regression.
RidgeRegressionWithSGD
```

3. Create the `LabeledPoint` array with the house price as the label:

```
scala> val points = Array(
LabeledPoint(1,Vectors.dense(5,3,1,2,1,3,2,2,1)),
LabeledPoint(2,Vectors.dense(9,8,8,9,7,9,8,7,9))
)
```

4. Create an RDD of the preceding data:

```
scala> val rdd = sc.parallelize(points)
```

5. Train a model using this data using 100 iterations. Here, the step size and regularization parameter have been set by hand :

```
scala> val model = RidgeRegressionWithSGD.train(rdd,100,0.02,2.0)
```

6. Check how many predictors have their coefficients set to zero:

```
scala> model.weights
org.apache.spark.mllib.linalg.Vector = [0.049805969577244584,0.029
883581746346748,0.009961193915448916,0.019922387830897833,0.009961
193915448916,0.029883581746346748,0.019922387830897833,0.019922387
830897833,0.009961193915448916]
```

As you can see, unlike lasso, ridge regression does not assign any predictor coefficients zero, but it does make some very close to zero.

8

Supervised Learning with MLlib – Classification

This chapter is divided into the following recipes:

- Doing classification using logistic regression
- Doing binary classification using SVM
- Doing classification using decision trees
- Doing classification using Random Forests
- Doing classification using Gradient Boosted Trees
- Doing classification with Naïve Bayes

Introduction

The classification problem is like the regression problem discussed in the previous chapter except that the outcome variable *y* takes only a few discrete values. In binary classification, *y* takes only two values: 0 or 1. You can also think of values that the response variable can take in classification as representing categories.

Doing classification using logistic regression

In classification, the response variable *y* has discreet values as opposed to continuous values. Some examples are e-mail (spam/non-spam), transactions (safe/fraudulent), and so on.

The *y* variable in the following equation can take on two values, 0 or 1:

$$y \in \{0,1\}$$

Here, 0 is referred to as a negative class and 1 means a positive class. Though we are calling them a positive or negative class, it is only for convenience's sake. Algorithms are neutral about this assignment.

Linear regression, though it works well for regression tasks, hits a few limitations for classification tasks. These include:

- The fitting process is very susceptible to outliers
- There is no guarantee that the hypothesis function *h(x)* will fit in the range 0 (negative class) to 1 (positive class)

Logistic regression guarantees that *h(x)* will fit between 0 and 1. Though logistic regression has the word regression in it, it is more of a misnomer and it is very much a classification algorithm:

$$1 \geq h(x) \geq 0$$

In linear regression, the hypothesis function is as follows:

$$h(x) = \theta^T x$$

In logistic regression, we slightly modify the hypothesis equation like this:

$$h(x) = g\left(\theta^T x\right)$$

The g function is called the **sigmoid function** or **logistic function** and is defined as follows for a real number *t*:

$$g(t) = \frac{1}{1+e^{-t}}$$

This is what the sigmoid function looks like as a graph:

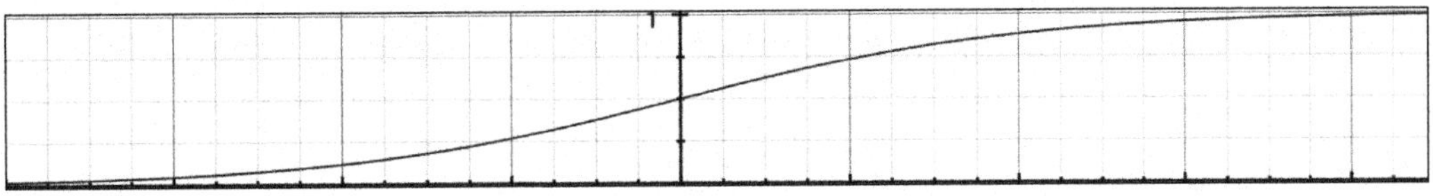

As you can see, as *t* approaches negative infinity, *g(t)* approaches 0 and, as *t* approaches infinity, *g(t)* approaches 1. So, this guarantees that the hypothesis function output will never fall out of the 0 to 1 range.

Now the hypothesis function can be rewritten as:

$$h(x) = \frac{1}{1+e^{-\theta^T x}}$$

h(x) is the estimated probability that *y = 1* for a given predictor *x*, so *h(x)* can also be rewritten as:

$$h(x) = P(y=1 \mid x;\theta)$$

In other words, the hypothesis function is showing the probability of *y* being 1 given feature matrix *x*, parameterized by θ. This probability can be any real number between 0 and 1 but our goal of classification does not allow us to have continuous values; we can only have two values 0 or 1 indicating the negative or positive class.

Let's say that we predict *y = 1* if $h(x) \geq 0.5$ and *y = 0* otherwise. If we look at the sigmoid function graph again, we realize that, when the $t \geq 0$ sigmoid function is ≥ 0.5, that is, for positive values of *t*, it will predict the positive class:

Since $h(x) = g(\theta^T x)$, this means for $\theta^T x \geq 0$ the positive class will be predicted. To better illustrate this, let's expand it to a non-matrix form for a bivariate case:

$$\theta^T x \geq 0$$

$$\theta_0 x_0 + \theta_1 x_1 + \theta_2 x_2 \geq 0$$

The plane represented by the equation $\theta_0 x_0 + \theta_1 x_1 + \theta_2 x_2 = 0$ will decide whether a given vector belongs to the positive class or negative class. This line is called the decision boundary.

This boundary does not have to be linear depending on the training set. If training data does not separate across a linear boundary, higher-level polynomial features can be added to facilitate it. An example can be to add two new features by squaring x1 and x2 as follows:

$$h(x)= \theta_0 x_0 + \theta_1 x_1 + \theta_2 x_2 + \theta_3 x_1^2 + \theta_4 x_2^2$$

Please note that, to the learning algorithm, this enhancement is exactly the same as the following equation:

$$h(x)= \theta_0 x_0 + \theta_1 x_1 + \theta_2 x_2 + \theta_3 x_3 + \theta_4 x_4$$

The learning algorithm will treat the introduction of polynomials just as another feature. This gives you great power in the fitting process. It means any complex decision boundary can be created with the right choice of polynomials and parameters.

Let's spend some time trying to understand how we choose the right value for parameters like we did in the case of linear regression. The cost function *J* in the case of linear regression was:

$$J(\theta_0,\theta_1)=\frac{1}{2m}\sum_{i=1}^{m}\left(h(x^i)-y^i\right)^2$$

As you know, we are averaging the cost in this cost function. Let's represent this in terms of cost term:

$$Cost\left(h(x^i)-y^i\right)=\frac{\left(h(x^i)-y^i\right)^2}{2}$$

$$J(\theta_0,\theta_1)=\frac{1}{m}\sum_{i=1}^{m}Cost\left(h(x^i)-y^i\right)$$

In other words, the cost term is the cost the algorithm has to pay if it predicts *h(x)* for the real response variable value *y*:

$$Cost\left(h(x)-y\right)=\frac{\left(h(x)-y\right)^2}{2}$$

This cost works fine for linear regression but, for logistic regression, this cost function is non-convex (that is, it leads to multiple local minimums) and we need to find a better convex way to estimate the cost.

The cost functions that work well for logistic regression are the following:

$$Cost\left(h(x),y\right) = -\log\left(h(x)\right) \quad //\text{for positive class}$$
$$Cost\left(h(x),y\right) = -\log\left(1-h(x)\right) \quad //\text{for negative class}$$

Let's put these two cost functions into one by combining the two:

$$Cost\left(h(x),y\right) = -y\log\left(h(x)\right) - (1-y)\log\left(1-h(x)\right)$$

Let's put back this cost function to *J*:

$$J(\theta) = -\frac{1}{m}\sum_{i=1}^{m}\left(y^i \log h\left(x^i\right) + \left(1-y^i\right)\log\left(1-h\left(x^i\right)\right)\right)$$

The goal would be to minimize the cost, that is, minimize the value of $J(\theta)$. This is done using the gradient descent algorithm. Spark has two classes that support logistic regression:

- `LogisticRegressionWithSGD`
- `LogisticRegressionWithLBFGS`

The `LogisticRegressionWithLBFGS` class is preferred as it eliminates the step of optimizing the step size.

Getting ready

In 2006, Suzuki, Tsurusaki, and Kodama did some research on the distribution of an endangered burrowing spider on different beaches in Japan (`https://www.jstage.jst.go.jp/article/asjaa/55/2/55_2_79/_pdf`).

Let's see some data about grain size and the presence of spiders:

Grain size (mm)	Spider present
0.245	Absent
0.247	Absent
0.285	Present
0.299	Present
0.327	Present
0.347	Present
0.356	Absent

Grain size (mm)	Spider present
0.36	Present
0.363	Absent
0.364	Present
0.398	Absent
0.4	Present
0.409	Absent
0.421	Present
0.432	Absent
0.473	Present
0.509	Present
0.529	Present
0.561	Absent
0.569	Absent
0.594	Present
0.638	Present
0.656	Present
0.816	Present
0.853	Present
0.938	Present
1.036	Present
1.045	Present

We will use this data to train the algorithm. Absent will be denoted as 0 and present will be denoted as 1.

How to do it...

1. Start the Spark shell:

```
$ spark-shell
```

2. Import statistics and related classes:

```
scala> import org.apache.spark.mllib.linalg.Vectors
scala> import org.apache.spark.mllib.regression.LabeledPoint
scala> import org.apache.spark.mllib.classification.
LogisticRegressionWithLBFGS
```

3. Create a `LabeledPoint` array with the presence or absence of spiders being the label:

```
scala> val points = Array(
LabeledPoint(0.0,Vectors.dense(0.245)),
LabeledPoint(0.0,Vectors.dense(0.247)),
LabeledPoint(1.0,Vectors.dense(0.285)),
LabeledPoint(1.0,Vectors.dense(0.299)),
LabeledPoint(1.0,Vectors.dense(0.327)),
LabeledPoint(1.0,Vectors.dense(0.347)),
LabeledPoint(0.0,Vectors.dense(0.356)),
LabeledPoint(1.0,Vectors.dense(0.36)),
LabeledPoint(0.0,Vectors.dense(0.363)),
LabeledPoint(1.0,Vectors.dense(0.364)),
LabeledPoint(0.0,Vectors.dense(0.398)),
LabeledPoint(1.0,Vectors.dense(0.4)),
LabeledPoint(0.0,Vectors.dense(0.409)),
LabeledPoint(1.0,Vectors.dense(0.421)),
LabeledPoint(0.0,Vectors.dense(0.432)),
LabeledPoint(1.0,Vectors.dense(0.473)),
LabeledPoint(1.0,Vectors.dense(0.509)),
LabeledPoint(1.0,Vectors.dense(0.529)),
LabeledPoint(0.0,Vectors.dense(0.561)),
LabeledPoint(0.0,Vectors.dense(0.569)),
LabeledPoint(1.0,Vectors.dense(0.594)),
LabeledPoint(1.0,Vectors.dense(0.638)),
LabeledPoint(1.0,Vectors.dense(0.656)),
LabeledPoint(1.0,Vectors.dense(0.816)),
LabeledPoint(1.0,Vectors.dense(0.853)),
LabeledPoint(1.0,Vectors.dense(0.938)),
LabeledPoint(1.0,Vectors.dense(1.036)),
LabeledPoint(1.0,Vectors.dense(1.045)))
```

4. Create an RDD of the preceding data:

```
scala> val spiderRDD = sc.parallelize(points)
```

5. Train a model using this data (intercept is the value when all predictors are zero):

```
scala> val lr = new LogisticRegressionWithLBFGS().
setIntercept(true)
scala> val model = lr.run(spiderRDD)
```

6. Predict the presence of spiders for grain size `0.938`:

```
scala> val predict = model.predict(Vectors.dense(0.938))
```

Doing binary classification using SVM

Classification is a technique to put data into different classes based on its utility. For example, an e-commerce company can apply two labels "will buy" or "will not buy" to potential visitors.

This classification is done by providing some already labeled data to machine learning algorithms called **training data**. The challenge is how to mark the boundary between two classes. Let's take a simple example as shown in the following figure:

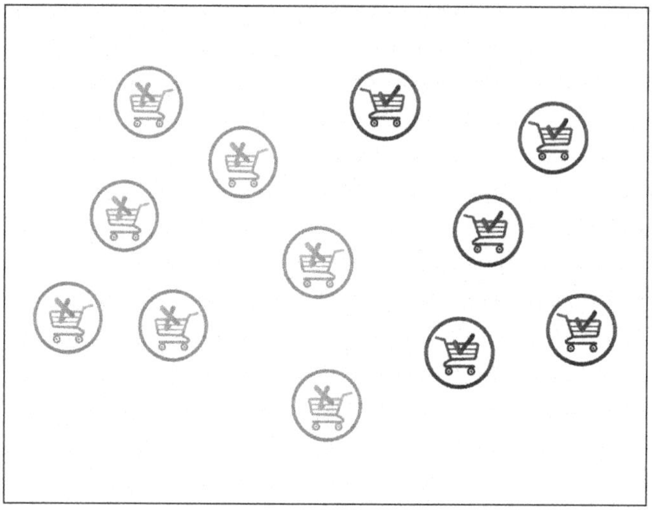

In the preceding case, we designated gray and black to the "will not buy" and "will buy" labels. Here, drawing a line between the two classes is as easy as follows:

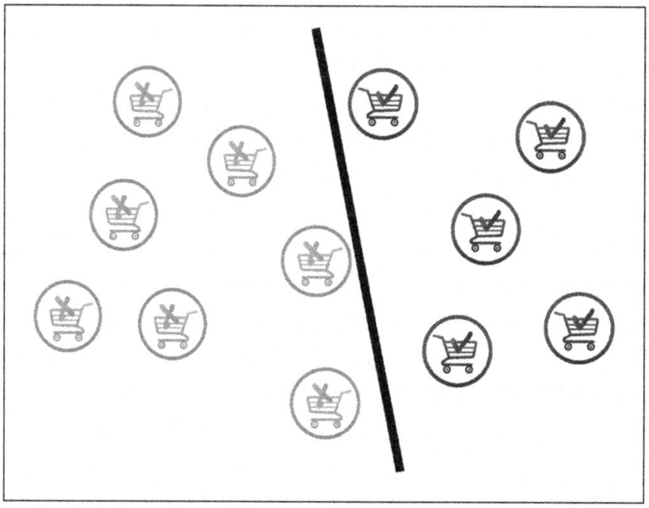

Is this the best we can do? Not really, let's try to do a better job. The black classifier is not really equidistant from the "will buy" and "will not buy" carts. Let's make a better attempt like the following:

Now this is looking good. This in fact is what the SVM algorithm does. You can see in the preceding diagram that in fact there are only three carts that decide the slope of the line: two black carts above the line, and one gray cart below the line. These carts are called **support vectors** and the rest of the carts, that is, the vectors, are irrelevant.

Sometimes it's not easy to draw a line and a curve may be needed to separate two classes like the following:

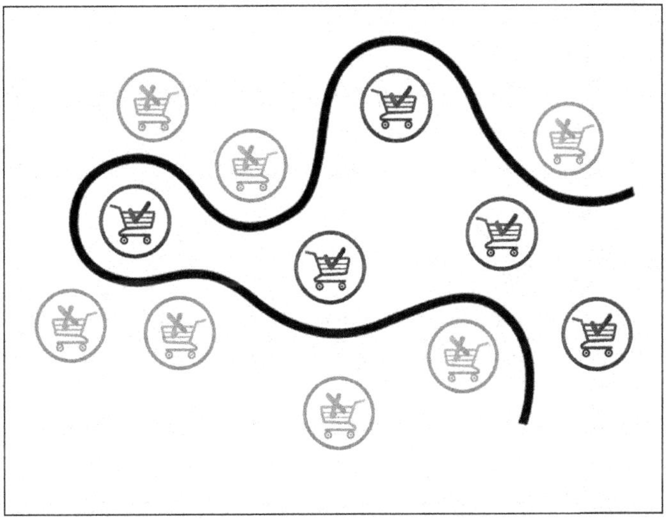

Sometimes even that is not enough. In that case, we need more than two dimensions to resolve the problem. Rather than a classified line, what we need is a hyperplane. In fact, whenever data is too cluttered, adding extra dimensions help to find a hyperplane to separate classes. The following diagram illustrates this:

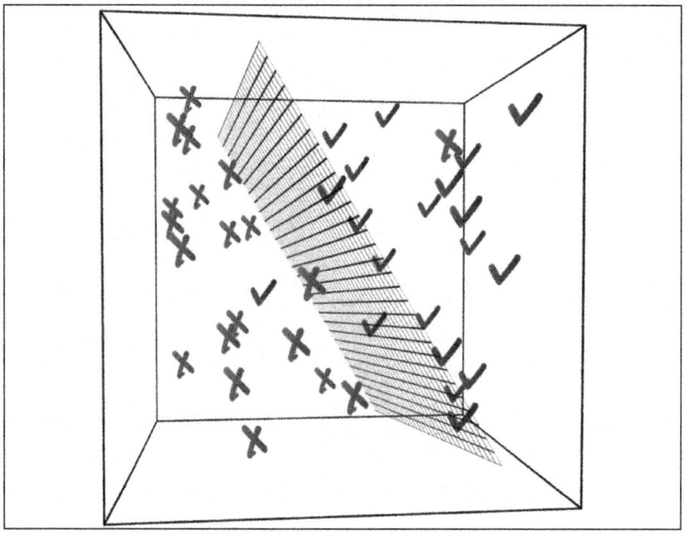

This does not mean that adding extra dimensions is always a good idea. Most of the time, our goal is to reduce dimensions and keep only the relevant dimensions/features. A whole set of algorithms is dedicated to dimensionality reduction; we will cover these in later chapters.

How to do it...

1. The Spark library comes loaded with sample `libsvm` data. We will use this and load the data into HDFS:

   ```
   $ hdfs dfs -put /opt/infoobjects/spark/data/mllib/sample_libsvm_
   data.txt /user/hduser/sample_libsvm_data.txt
   ```

2. Start the Spark shell:

   ```
   $ spark-shell
   ```

3. Perform the required imports:

   ```
   scala> import org.apache.spark.mllib.classification.SVMWithSGD
   scala> import org.apache.spark.mllib.evaluation.
   BinaryClassificationMetrics
   scala> import org.apache.spark.mllib.regression.LabeledPoint
   scala> import org.apache.spark.mllib.linalg.Vectors
   scala> import org.apache.spark.mllib.util.MLUtils
   ```

4. Load the data as the RDD:

```
scala> val svmData = MLUtils.loadLibSVMFile(sc,"sample_libsvm_
data.txt")
```

5. Count the number of records:

```
scala> svmData.count
```

6. Now let's divide the dataset into half training data and half testing data:

```
scala> val trainingAndTest = svmData.randomSplit(Array(0.5,0.5))
```

7. Assign the `training` and `test` data:

```
scala> val trainingData = trainingAndTest(0)
scala> val testData = trainingAndTest(1)
```

8. Train the algorithm and build the model for 100 iterations (you can try different iterations but you will see that, at a certain point, the results start to converge and that is a good number to choose):

```
scala> val model = SVMWithSGD.train(trainingData,100)
```

9. Now we can use this model to predict a label for any dataset. Let's predict the label for the first point in the test data:

```
scala> val label = model.predict(testData.first.features)
```

10. Let's create a tuple that has the first value as a prediction for test data and a second value actual label, which will help us compute the accuracy of our algorithm:

```
scala> val predictionsAndLabels = testData.map( r => (model.
predict(r.features),r.label))
```

11. You can count how many records have prediction and actual label mismatches:

```
scala> predictionsAndLabels.filter(p => p._1 != p._2).count
```

Doing classification using decision trees

Decision trees are the most intuitive among machine learning algorithms. We use decision trees in daily life all the time.

Decision tree algorithms have a lot of useful features:

- Easy to understand and interpret
- Work with both categorical and continuous features
- Work with missing features
- Do not require feature scaling

Decision tree algorithms work in an upside-down order in which an expression containing a feature is evaluated at every level and that splits the dataset into two categories. We'll help you understand this with the simple example of a dumb charade, which most of us played in college. I guessed an animal and asked my coworker ask me questions to work out my choice. Here's how her questioning went:

Q1: Is it a big animal?

A: Yes

Q2: Does this animal live more than 40 years?

A: Yes

Q3: Is this animal an elephant?

A: Yes

This is an obviously oversimplified case in which she knew I had postulated an elephant (what else would you guess in a Big Data world?). Let's expand this example to include some more animals as in the following figure (grayed boxes are classes):

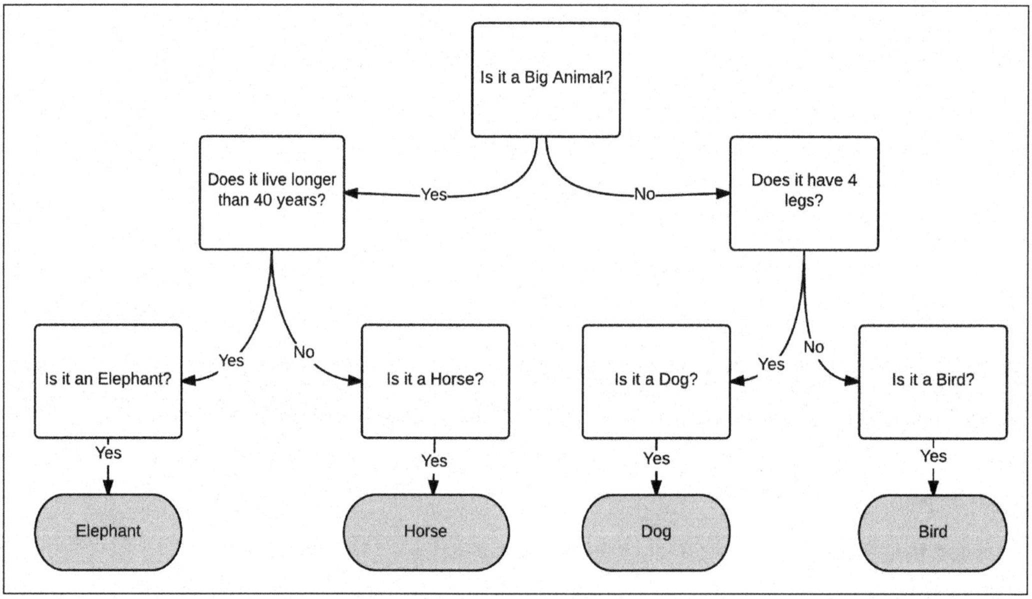

The preceding example is a case of multiclass classification. In this recipe, we are going to focus on binary classification.

Getting ready

Whenever our son has to take tennis lessons in the morning, the night before the instructor checks the weather reports and decides whether the next morning would be good to play tennis. This recipe will use this example to build a decision tree.

Let's decide on the features of weather that affect the decision whether to play tennis in the morning or not:

- Rain
- Wind speed
- Temperature

Let's build a table of the different combinations:

Rain	**Windy**	**Temperature**	**Play tennis?**
Yes	Yes	Hot	No
Yes	Yes	Normal	No
Yes	Yes	Cool	No
No	Yes	Hot	No
No	Yes	Cool	No
No	No	Hot	Yes
No	No	Normal	Yes
No	No	Cool	No

Now how do we build a decision tree? We can start with one of three features: rain, windy, or temperature. The rule is to start with a feature so that the maximum information gain is possible.

On a rainy day, as you can see in the table, other features do not matter and there is no play. The same is true for high wind velocity.

Decision trees, like most other algorithms, take feature values only as double values. So, let's do the mapping:

$$Rain\{Yes, No\} => \{2.0, 1.0\}$$
$$Windy\{Yes, No\} => \{2.0, 1.0\}$$
$$Temperature\{Hot, Normal, Cold\} => \{3.0, 2.0, 1.0\}$$

The positive class is 1.0 and the negative class is 0.0. Let's load the data using the CSV format using the first value as a label:

```
$vi tennis.csv
0.0,1.0,1.0,2.0
0.0,1.0,1.0,1.0
0.0,1.0,1.0,0.0
0.0,0.0,1.0,2.0
0.0,0.0,1.0,0.0
1.0,0.0,0.0,2.0
1.0,0.0,0.0,1.0
0.0,0.0,0.0,0.0
```

How to do it...

1. Start the Spark shell:

   ```
   $ spark-shell
   ```

2. Perform the required imports:

   ```
   scala> import org.apache.spark.mllib.tree.DecisionTree
   scala> import org.apache.spark.mllib.regression.LabeledPoint
   scala> import org.apache.spark.mllib.linalg.Vectors
   scala> import org.apache.spark.mllib.tree.configuration.Algo._
   scala> import org.apache.spark.mllib.tree.impurity.Entropy
   ```

3. Load the file:

   ```
   scala> val data = sc.textFile("tennis.csv")
   ```

4. Parse the data and load it into `LabeledPoint`:

   ```
   scala> val parsedData = data.map {
   line =>  val parts = line.split(',').map(_.toDouble)
    LabeledPoint(parts(0), Vectors.dense(parts.tail)) }
   ```

5. Train the algorithm with this data:

   ```
   scala> val model = DecisionTree.train(parsedData, Classification,
   Entropy, 3)
   ```

6. Create a vector for no rain, high wind, and a cool temperature:

   ```
   scala> val v=Vectors.dense(0.0,1.0,0.0)
   ```

7. Predict whether tennis should be played:

   ```
   scala> model.predict(v)
   ```

How it works...

Let's draw the decision tree for tennis that we created in this recipe:

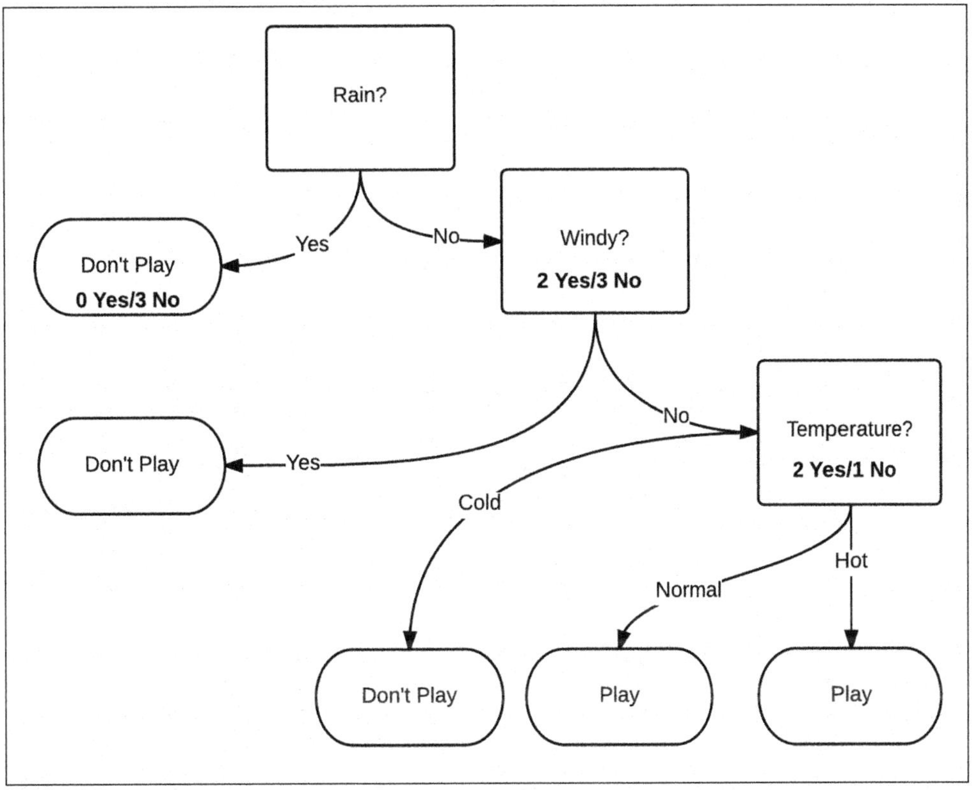

This model has a depth of three levels. Which attribute to select depends upon how we can maximize information gain. The way it is measured is by measuring the purity of the split. Purity means that, whether or not certainty is increasing, then that given dataset will be considered as positive or negative. In this example, this equates to whether the chances of play are increasing or the chances of not playing are increasing.

Purity is measured using entropy. Entropy is a measure of disorder in a system. In this context, it is easier to understand it as a measure of uncertainty:

$$Entropy(S) = -p_+ log_2 p_+ - p_- log_2 p_-$$

The highest level of purity is 0 and the lowest is 1. Let's try to determine the purity using the formula.

When rain is yes, the probability of playing tennis is *p+* is 0/3 = 0. The probability of not playing tennis *p_* is 3/3 = 1:

$$Entropy(S) = -0 - 1log1 = 0$$

This is a pure set.

When rain is a no, the probability of playing tennis is *p+* is 2/5 = 0.4. The probability of not playing tennis *p_* is 3/5 = 0.6:

$$\begin{aligned} Entropy(S) &= -0.4log_2 04 - 0.6log_2 0.6 \\ &= -0.4 \times (-1.32) - 0.6 \times (-0.736) \\ &= 0.528 + 0.4416 \\ &= 0.967 \end{aligned}$$

This is almost an impure set. The most impure would be the case where the probability is 0.5.

Spark uses three measures to determine impurity:

- Gini impurity (classification)
- Entropy (classification)
- Variance (regression)

Information gain is the difference between the parent node impurity and the weighted sum of two child node impurities. Let's look at the first split, which partitions data of size eight to two datasets of size three (left) and five (right). Let's call the first split *s1*, the parent node *rain*, the left child *no rain*, and the right child *wind*. So the information gain would be:

$$IG(rain, s1) = Impurity(rain) - \left(\frac{N_{no\ rain}}{N_{rain}}\right) Impurity(no\ rain) - \left(\frac{N_{wind}}{N_{rain}}\right) Impurity(wind)$$

As we calculated impurity for *no rain* and *wind* already for the entropy, let's calculate the entropy for *rain*:

$$\begin{aligned} Entropy(rain) &= -\left(\frac{2}{8}\right) log_2 \left(\frac{2}{8}\right) - \left(\frac{6}{8}\right) log_2 \left(\frac{6}{8}\right) \\ &= -\left(\frac{1}{4}\right) \times (-2) - \left(\frac{3}{4}\right) \times (-0.41) \\ &= 0.8 \end{aligned}$$

Let's calculate the information gain now:

$$IG(rain, s1) = Impurity(rain) - \left(\frac{N_{no\ rain}}{N_{rain}}\right) Impurity(no\ rain) - \left(\frac{N_{wind}}{N_{rain}}\right) Impurity(wind)$$

$$= 0.8 - \left(\frac{5}{8}\right) \times 0.967$$

$$= 0.2$$

So the information gain is 0.2 in the first split. Is this the best we can achieve? Let's see what our algorithm comes up with. First, let's find out the depth of the tree:

```
scala> model.depth
Int = 2
```

Here, the depth is `2` compared to the `3` we intuitively built, so this model seems to be better optimized. Let's look at the structure of the tree:

```
scala> model.toDebugString
String =  "DecisionTreeModel classifier of depth 2 with 5 nodes
If (feature 1 <= 0.0)
   If (feature 2 <= 0.0)
     Predict: 0.0
   Else (feature 2 > 0.0)
     Predict: 1.0
Else (feature 1 > 0.0)
    Predict: 0.0
```

Let's build it visually to get a better understanding:

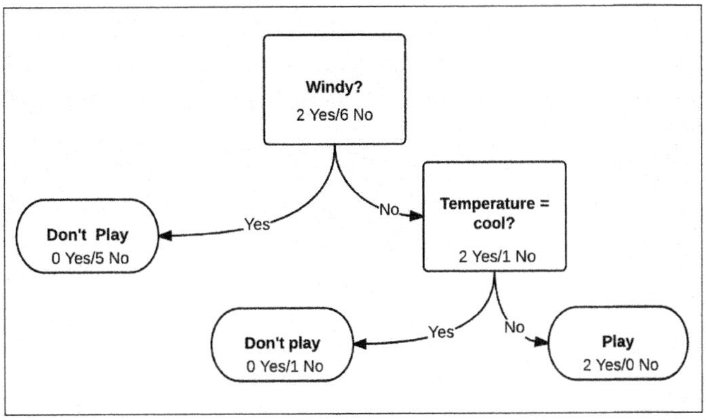

We will not go into detail here as we already did this with the previous model. We will straightaway calculate the information gain: 0.44

As you can see in this case, the information gain is 0.44, which is more than double the first model.

If you look at the second level nodes, the impurity is zero. In this case, it is great as we got it at a depth of 2. Image a situation in which the depth is 50. In that case, the decision tree would work well for training data and would do badly for test data. This situation is called **overfitting**.

One solution to avoid overfitting is pruning. You divide your training data into two sets: the training set and validation set. You train the model using the training set. Now you test with the model against the validation set by slowly removing the left nodes. If removing the leaf node (which is mostly a singleton—that is, it contains only one data point) improves the performance of the model, this leaf node is pruned from the model.

Doing classification using Random Forests

Sometimes one decision tree is not enough, so a set of decision trees is used to produce more powerful models. These are called **ensemble learning algorithms**. Ensemble learning algorithms are not limited to using decision trees as base models.

The most popular among the ensemble learning algorithms is Random Forest. In Random Forest, rather than growing one single tree, *K* trees are grown. Every tree is given a random subset *S* of training data. To add a twist to it, every tree only uses a subset of features. When it comes to making predictions, a majority vote is done on the trees and that becomes the prediction.

Let's explain this with an example. The goal is to make a prediction for a given person about whether he/she has good credit or bad credit.

To do this, we will provide labeled training data—that is, in this case, a person with features and labels whether he/she has good credit or bad credit. Now we do not want to create feature bias so we will provide a randomly selected set of features. There is another reason to provide a randomly selected subset of features and that is because most real-world data has hundreds if not thousands of features. Text classification algorithms, for example, typically have 50k-100k features.

In this case, to add flavor to the story we are not going to provide features, but we will ask different people why they think a person has good or bad credit. Now by definition, different people are exposed to different features (sometimes overlapping) of a person, which gives us the same functionality as randomly selected features.

Our first example is Jack who carries a label "bad credit." We will start with Joey who works at Jack's favorite bar, the Elephant Bar. The only way a person can deduce why a given label was given is by asking yes/no questions. Let's see what Joey says:

Q1: Does Jack tip well? (Feature: generosity)

A: No

Q2: Does Jack spend at least $60 per visit? (Feature: spendthrift)

A: Yes

Q3: Does he tend to get into bar fights even at the smallest provocation? (Feature: volatile)

A: Yes

That explains why Jack has bad credit.

We now ask Jack's girlfriend, Stacey:

Q1: When we hangout, does Jack always cover the bill? (Feature: generosity)

A: No

Q2: Has Jack paid me back the $500 he owes me? (Feature: responsibility)

A: No

Q3: Does he overspend sometimes just to show off? (Feature: spendthrift)

A: Yes

That explains why Jack has bad credit.

We now ask Jack's best friend George:

Q1: When Jack and I hang out at my apartment, does he clean up after himself? (Feature: organized)

A: No

Q2: Did Jack arrive empty-handed during my Super Bowl potluck? (Feature: care)

A: Yes

Q3: Has he used the "I forgot my wallet at home" excuse for me to cover his tab at restaurants? (Feature: responsibility)

A: Yes

That explains why Jack has bad credit.

Now we talk about Jessica who has good credit. Let's ask Stacey who happens to be Jessica's sister:

Q1: Whenever I run short of money, does Jessica offer to help? (Feature: generosity)

A: Yes

Q2: Does Jessica pay her bills on time? (Feature: responsibility)

A: Yes

Q3: Does Jessica offer to babysit my child? (Feature: care)

A: Yes

That explains why Jessica has good credit.

Now we ask George who happens to be her husband:

Q1: Does Jessica keep the house tidy? (Feature: organized)

A: Yes

Q2: Does she expect expensive gifts? (Feature: spendthrift)

A: No

Q3: Does she get upset when you forget to mow the lawn? (Feature: volatile)

A: No

That explains why Jessica has good credit.

Now let's ask Joey, the bartender at the Elephant Bar:

Q1: Whenever she comes to the bar with friends, is she mostly the designated driver? (Feature: responsible)

A: Yes

Q2: Does she always take leftovers home? (Feature: spendthrift)

A: Yes

Q3: Does she tip well? (Feature: generosity)

A: Yes

The way Random Forest works is that it does random selection on two levels:

- A subset of the data
- A subset of features to split that data

Both these subsets can overlap.

In our example, we have six features and we are going to assign three features to each tree. This way, there is a good chance we will have an overlap.

Let's add eight more people to our training dataset:

Names	**Label**	**Generosity**	**Responsibility**	**Care**	**Organization**	**Spendthrift**	**Volatile**
Jack	0	0	0	0	0	1	1
Jessica	1	1	1	1	1	0	0
Jenny	0	0	0	1	0	1	1
Rick	1	1	1	0	1	0	0
Pat	0	0	0	0	0	1	1
Jeb	1	1	1	1	0	0	0
Jay	1	0	1	1	1	0	0
Nat	0	1	0	0	0	1	1
Ron	1	0	1	1	1	0	0
Mat	0	1	0	0	0	1	1

Getting ready

Let's put the data we created into the `libsvm` format in the following file:

`rf_libsvm_data.txt`

```
0 5:1 6:1
1 1:1 2:1 3:1 4:1
0 3:1 5:1 6:1
1 1:1 2:1 4:1
0 5:1 6:1
1 1:1 2:1 3:1 4:1
0 1:1 5:1 6:1
1 2:1 3:1 4:1
0 1:1 5:1 6:1
```

Now upload it to HDFS:

```
$ hdfs dfs -put rf_libsvm_data.txt
```

How to do it...

1. Start the Spark shell:

   ```
   $ spark-shell
   ```

2. Perform the required imports:

   ```
   scala> import org.apache.spark.mllib.tree.RandomForest
   scala> import org.apache.spark.mllib.tree.configuration.Strategy
   scala> import org.apache.spark.mllib.util.MLUtils
   ```

3. Load and parse the data:

   ```
   scala> val data =
     MLUtils.loadLibSVMFile(sc, "rf_libsvm_data.txt")
   ```

4. Split the data into the `training` and `test` datasets:

   ```
   scala> val splits = data.randomSplit(Array(0.7, 0.3))
   scala> val (trainingData, testData) = (splits(0), splits(1))
   ```

5. Create a classification as a tree strategy (Random Forest also supports regression):

   ```
   scala> val treeStrategy = Strategy.defaultStrategy("Classificati
   on")
   ```

6. Train the model:

   ```
   scala> val model = RandomForest.trainClassifier(trainingData,
     treeStrategy, numTrees=3, featureSubsetStrategy="auto", seed =
   12345)
   ```

7. Evaluate the model on test instances and compute the test error:

   ```
   scala> val testErr = testData.map { point =>
     val prediction = model.predict(point.features)
     if (point.label == prediction) 1.0 else 0.0
   }.mean()
   scala> println("Test Error = " + testErr)
   ```

8. Check the model:

   ```
   scala> println("Learned Random Forest:n" + model.toDebugString)
   Learned Random Forest:nTreeEnsembleModel classifier with 3 trees
       Tree 0:
   ```

```
        If (feature 5 <= 0.0)
          Predict: 1.0
        Else (feature 5 > 0.0)
          Predict: 0.0
          Tree 1:
            If (feature 3 <= 0.0)
             Predict: 0.0
           Else (feature 3 > 0.0)
            Predict: 1.0
         Tree 2:
            If (feature 0 <= 0.0)
             Predict: 0.0
           Else (feature 0 > 0.0)
            Predict: 1.0
```

How it works...

As you can see in such a small example, three trees are using different features. In real-world use cases with thousands of features and training data, this would not happen, but most of the trees would differ in how they look at features and the vote of the majority will win. Please remember that, in the case of regression, averaging is done over trees to get a final value.

Doing classification using Gradient Boosted Trees

Another ensemble learning algorithm is **Gradient Boosted Trees** (**GBTs**). GBTs train one tree at a time, where each new tree improves upon the shortcomings of previously trained trees.

As GBTs train one tree at a time, they can take longer than Random Forest.

Getting ready

We are going to use the same data we used in the previous recipe.

How to do it...

1. Start the Spark shell:

   ```
   $ spark-shell
   ```

2. Perform the required imports:

```
scala> import org.apache.spark.mllib.tree.GradientBoostedTrees
scala> import org.apache.spark.mllib.tree.configuration.
BoostingStrategy
scala> import org.apache.spark.mllib.util.MLUtils
```

3. Load and parse the data:

```
scala> val data =
  MLUtils.loadLibSVMFile(sc, "rf_libsvm_data.txt")
```

4. Split the data into `training` and `test` datasets:

```
scala> val splits = data.randomSplit(Array(0.7, 0.3))
scala> val (trainingData, testData) = (splits(0), splits(1))
```

5. Create a classification as a boosting strategy and set the number of iterations to `3`:

```
scala> val boostingStrategy =
  BoostingStrategy.defaultParams("Classification")
scala> boostingStrategy.numIterations = 3
```

6. Train the model:

```
scala> val model = GradientBoostedTrees.train(trainingData,
boostingStrategy)
```

7. Evaluate the model on the test instances and compute the test error:

```
scala> val testErr = testData.map { point =>
  val prediction = model.predict(point.features)
  if (point.label == prediction) 1.0 else 0.0
}.mean()
scala> println("Test Error = " + testErr)
```

8. Check the model:

```
scala> println("Learned Random Forest:n" + model.toDebugString)
```

In this case, the accuracy of the model is 0.9, which is less than what we got in the case of Random Forest.

Doing classification with Naïve Bayes

Let's consider building an e-mail spam filter using machine learning. Here we are interested in two classes: spam for unsolicited messages and non-spam for regular emails:

$$y \in \{0,1\}$$

The first challenge is that, when given an e-mail, how do we represent it as feature vector x. An e-mail is just bunch of text or a collection of words (therefore, this problem domain falls into a broader category called **text classification**). Let's represent an e-mail with a feature vector with the length equal to the size of the dictionary. If a given word in a dictionary appears in an e-mail, the value will be 1; otherwise 0. Let's build a vector representing e-mail with the content *online pharmacy sale*:

$$x = \begin{bmatrix} 0 \\ 0 \\ \dots \\ 1 \\ \dots \\ 1 \\ \dots \\ 1 \\ \dots \end{bmatrix} \begin{array}{c} a \\ aard-vark \\ \dots \\ online \\ \dots \\ pharmacy \\ \dots \\ sale \\ \dots \end{array}$$

The dictionary of words in this feature vector is called *vocabulary* and the dimensions of the vector are the same as the size of vocabulary. If the vocabulary size is 10,000, the possible values in this feature vector will be 210,000.

Our goal is to model the probability of x given *y*. To model *P(x|y)*, we will make a strong assumption, and that assumption is that x's are conditionally independent. This assumption is called the **Naïve Bayes assumption** and the algorithm based on this assumption is called the **Naïve Bayes classifier**.

For example, for *y =1*, which means spam, the probability of "online" appearing and "pharmacy appearing" are independent. This is a strong assumption that has nothing to do with reality but works out really well when it comes to getting good predictions.

Getting ready

Spark comes bundled with a sample dataset to use with Naïve Bayes. Let's load this dataset to HDFS:

```
$ hdfs dfs -put /opt/infoobjects/spark/data/mllib/sample_naive_bayes_
data.txt
 sample_naive_bayes_data.txt
```

How to do it...

1. Start the Spark shell:

   ```
   $ spark-shell
   ```

2. Perform the required imports:

   ```
   scala> import org.apache.spark.mllib.classification.NaiveBayes
   scala> import org.apache.spark.mllib.linalg.Vectors
   scala> import org.apache.spark.mllib.regression.LabeledPoint
   ```

3. Load the data into RDD:

   ```
   scala> val data = sc.textFile("sample_naive_bayes_data.txt")
   ```

4. Parse the data into `LabeledPoint`:

   ```
   scala> val parsedData = data.map { line =>
     val parts = line.split(',')
     LabeledPoint(parts(0).toDouble, Vectors.dense(parts(1).split('
   ').map(_.toDouble)))
   }
   ```

5. Split the data half and half into the `training` and `test` datasets:

   ```
   scala> val splits = parsedData.randomSplit(Array(0.5, 0.5), seed =
   11L)
   scala> val training = splits(0)
   scala> val test = splits(1)
   ```

6. Train the model with the `training` dataset:

   ```
   val model = NaiveBayes.train(training, lambda = 1.0)
   ```

7. Predict the label of the `test` dataset:

   ```
   val predictionAndLabel = test.map(p => (model.predict(p.features),
   p.label))
   ```

9
Unsupervised Learning with MLlib

This chapter will cover how we can do unsupervised learning using MLlib, Spark's machine learning library.

This chapter is divided into the following recipes:

- Clustering using k-means
- Dimensionality reduction with principal component analysis
- Dimensionality reduction with singular value decomposition

Introduction

The following is Wikipedia's definition of unsupervised learning:

> *"In machine learning, the problem of unsupervised learning is that of trying to find hidden structure in unlabeled data."*

In contrast to supervised learning where we have labeled data to train an algorithm, in unsupervised learning we ask the algorithm to find a structure on its own. Let's take a look at the following sample dataset:

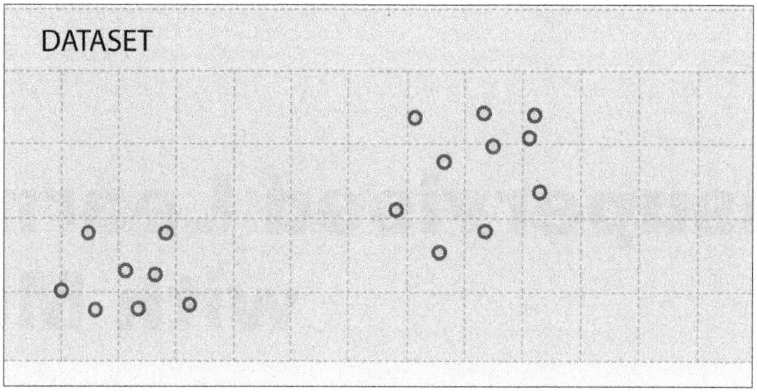

As you can see from the preceding graph, the data points are forming two clusters as follows:

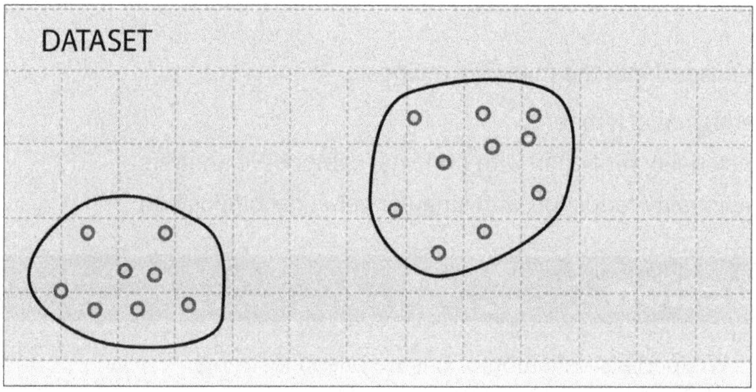

In fact, clustering is the most common type of unsupervised learning algorithm.

Clustering using k-means

Cluster analysis or clustering is the process of grouping data into multiple groups so that the data in one group is similar to the data in other groups.

The following are a few examples where clustering is used:

- **Market segmentation**: Dividing the target market into multiple segments so that the needs of each segment can be served better
- **Social network analysis**: Finding a coherent group of people in the social network for ad targeting through a social networking site such as Facebook

- **Data center computing clusters**: Putting a set of computers together to improve performance
- **Astronomical data analysis**: Understanding astronomical data and events such as galaxy formations
- **Real estate**: Identifying neighborhoods based on similar features
- **Text analysis**: Dividing text documents, such as novels or essays, into genres

The k-means algorithm is best illustrated using imagery, so let's look at our sample figure again:

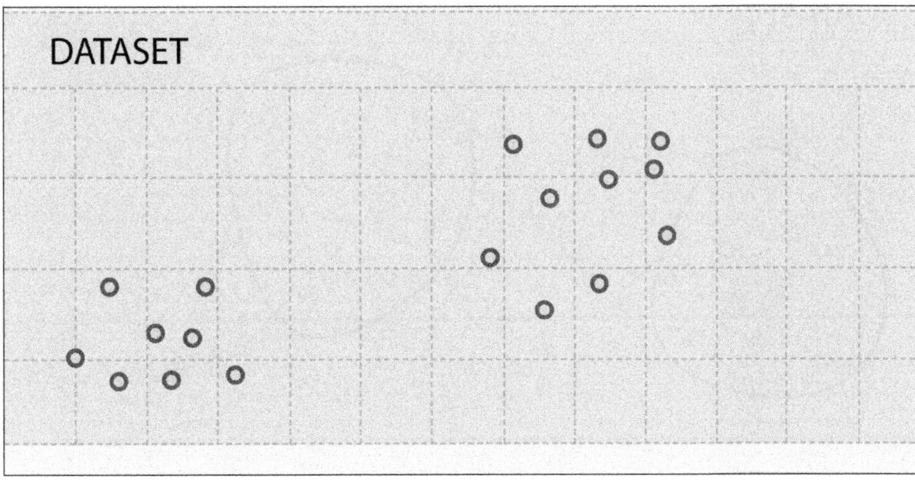

The first step in k-means is to randomly select two points called **cluster centroids**:

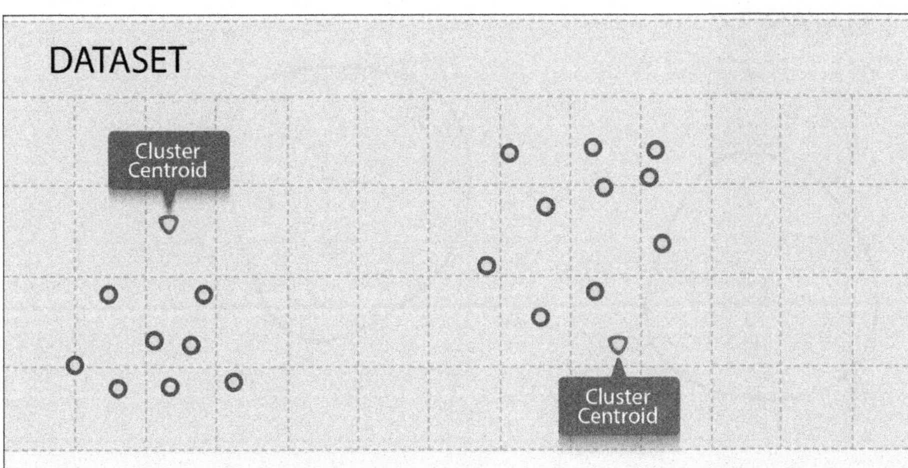

The k-means algorithm is an iterative algorithm and works in two steps:

- **Cluster assignment step**: This algorithm will go through each data point and, depending upon which centroid it is nearer to, it will be assigned that centroid and, in turn, the cluster it represents
- **Move centroid step**: This algorithm will take each centroid and move it to the mean of the data points in the cluster

Let's see how our data looks after the cluster assignment:

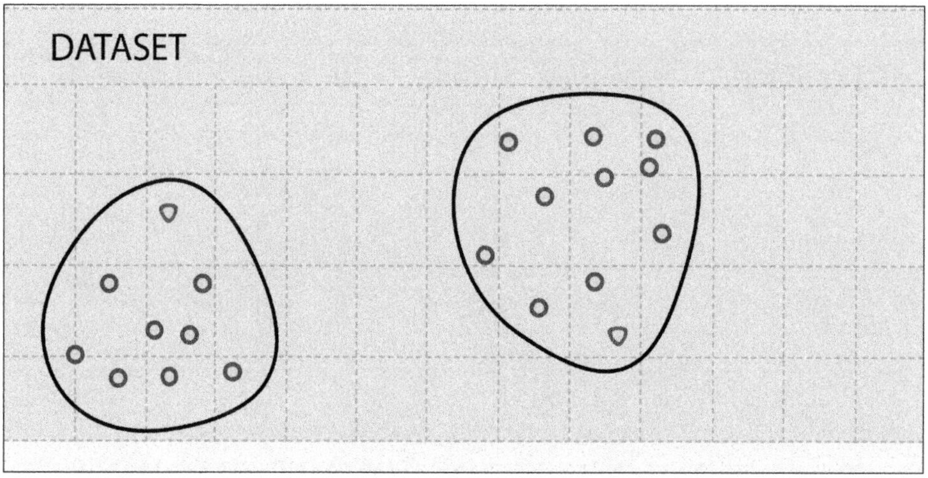

Now let's move the cluster centroids to the mean value of the data points in a cluster, as follows:

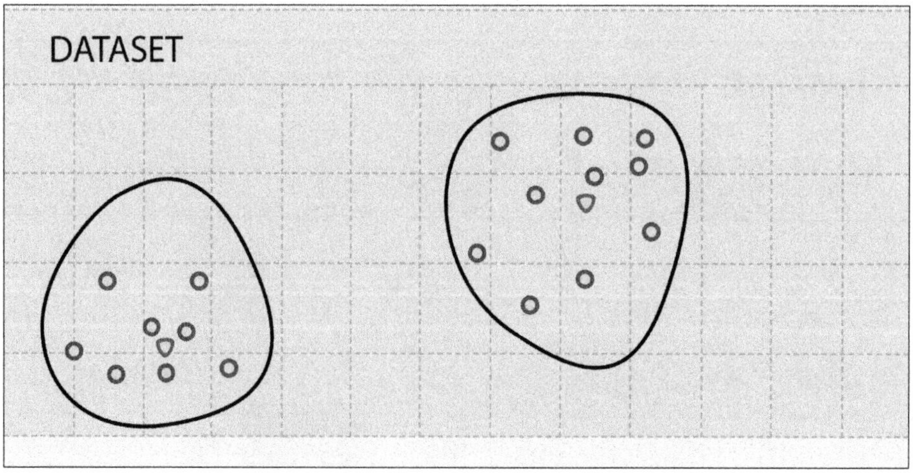

In this case, one iteration is enough and further iterations will not move the cluster centroids. For most real data, multiple iterations are required to move the centroid to the final position.

The k-means algorithm takes a number of clusters as input.

Getting ready

Let's use some different housing data from the City of Saratoga, CA. This time, we are going to take lot size and house price:

Lot size	House price (in $1,000)
12839	2405
10000	2200
8040	1400
13104	1800
10000	2351
3049	795
38768	2725
16250	2150
43026	2724
44431	2675
40000	2930
1260	870
15000	2210
10032	1145
12420	2419
69696	2750
12600	2035
10240	1150
876	665
8125	1430
11792	1920
1512	1230
1276	975
67518	2400
9810	1725
6324	2300
12510	1700

Lot size	House price (in $1,000)
15616	1915
15476	2278
13390	2497.5
1158	725
2000	870
2614	730
13433	2050
12500	3330
15750	1120
13996	4100
10450	1655
7500	1550
12125	2100
14500	2100
10000	1175
10019	2047.5
48787	3998
53579	2688
10788	2251
11865	1906

Let's convert this data into a **comma-separated value** (**CSV**) file called `saratoga.csv` and draw it as a scatter plot:

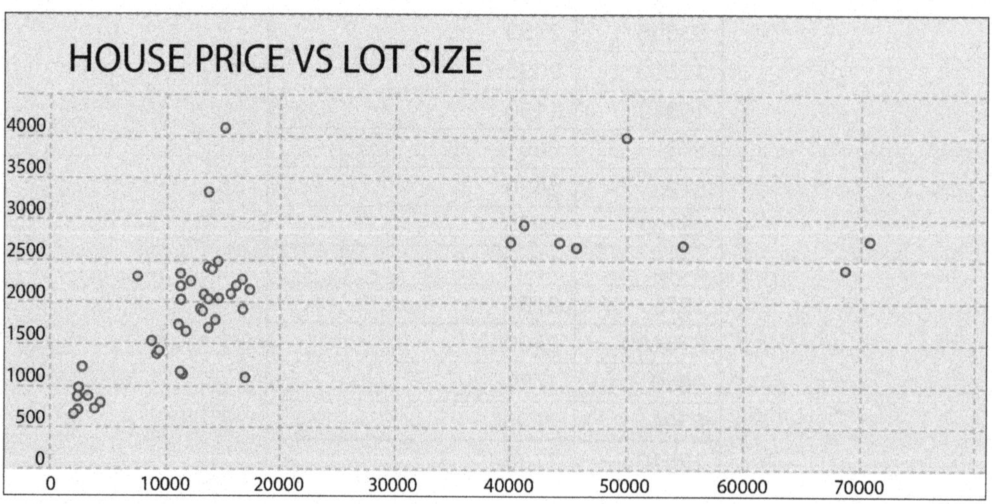

Finding a number of clusters is a tricky task. Here, we have the advantage of visual inspection, which is not available for data on hyperplanes (more than three dimensions). Let's roughly divide the data into four clusters as follows:

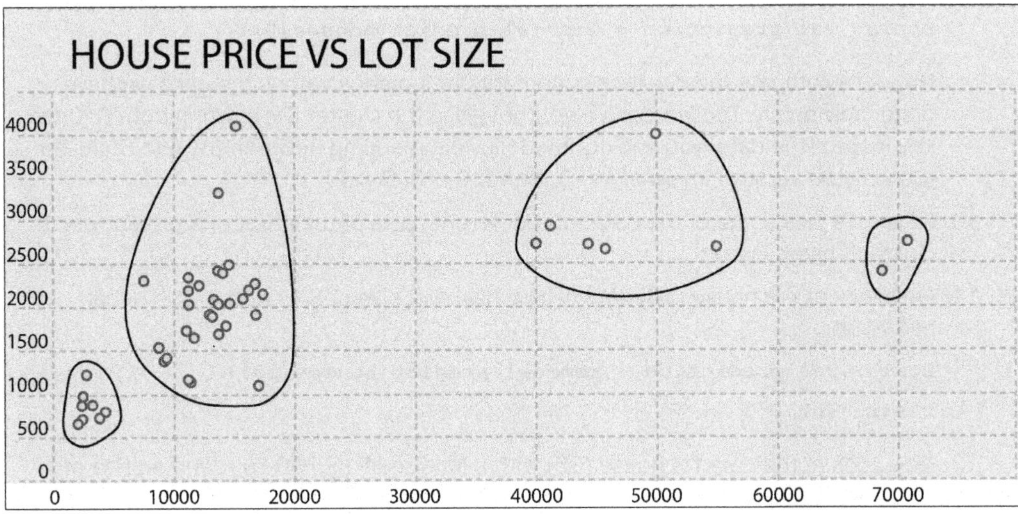

We will run the k-means algorithm to do the same and see how close our results come.

How to do it...

1. Load `saratagaga.csv` to HDFS:

   ```
   $ hdfs dfs -put saratoga.csv saratoga.csv
   ```

2. Start the Spark shell:

   ```
   $ spark-shell
   ```

3. Import statistics and related classes:

   ```
   scala> import org.apache.spark.mllib.linalg.Vectors
   scala> import org.apache.spark.mllib.clustering.KMeans
   ```

4. Load `saratoga.csv` as an RDD:

   ```
   scala> val data = sc.textFile("saratoga.csv")
   ```

5. Transform the data into an RDD of dense vectors:

   ```
   scala> val parsedData = data.map( line => Vectors.dense(line.
   split(',').map(_.toDouble)))
   ```

6. Train the model for four clusters and five iterations:

   ```
   scala> val kmmodel= KMeans.train(parsedData,4,5)
   ```

7. Collect `parsedData` as a local scala collection:

```
scala> val houses = parsedData.collect
```

8. Predict the cluster for the 0th element:

```
scala> val prediction = kmmodel.predict(houses(0))
```

9. Now let's compare the cluster assignments by k-means versus the ones we have done individually. The k-means algorithm gives the cluster IDs starting from 0. Once you inspect the data, you find out the following mapping between the A to D cluster IDs we gave versus k-means: A=>3, B=>1, C=>0, D=>2.
10. Now, let's pick some of the data from different parts of the chart and predict which cluster it belongs to.
11. Let's look at the house (18) data, which has a lot size of 876 sq ft and is priced at $665K:

```
scala> val prediction = kmmodel.predict(houses(18))
resxx: Int = 3
```

12. Now, look at the data for house (35) with a lot size of 15,750 sq ft and a price of $1.12 million:

```
scala> val prediction = kmmodel.predict(houses(35))
resxx: Int = 1
```

13. Now look at the house (6) data, which has a lot size of 38,768 sq ft and is priced at $2.725 million:

```
scala> val prediction = kmmodel.predict(houses(6))
resxx: Int = 0
```

14. Now look at the house (15) data, which has a lot size of 69,696 sq ft and is priced at $2.75 million:

```
scala>  val prediction = kmmodel.predict(houses(15))
resxx: Int = 2
```

You can test the prediction capability with more data. Let's do some neighborhood analysis to see what meaning these clusters carry. Most of the houses in cluster 3 are near downtown. The cluster 2 houses are on hilly terrain.

In this example, we dealt with a very small set of features; common sense and visual inspection would also lead us to the same conclusions. The beauty of the k-means algorithm is that it does the clustering on the data with an unlimited number of features. It is a great tool to use when you have a raw data and would like to know the patterns in that data.

Dimensionality reduction with principal component analysis

Dimensionality reduction is the process of reducing the number of dimensions or features. A lot of real data contains a very high number of features. It is not uncommon to have thousands of features. Now, we need to drill down to features that matter.

Dimensionality reduction serves several purposes such as:

- Data compression
- Visualization

When the number of dimensions is reduced, it reduces the disk footprint and memory footprint. Last but not least; it helps algorithms to run much faster. It also helps reduce highly correlated dimensions to one.

Humans can only visualize three dimensions, but data can have a much higher number of dimensions. Visualization can help find hidden patterns in the data. Dimensionality reduction helps visualization by compacting multiple features into one.

The most popular algorithm for dimensionality reduction is **principal component analysis** (**PCA**).

Let's look at the following dataset:

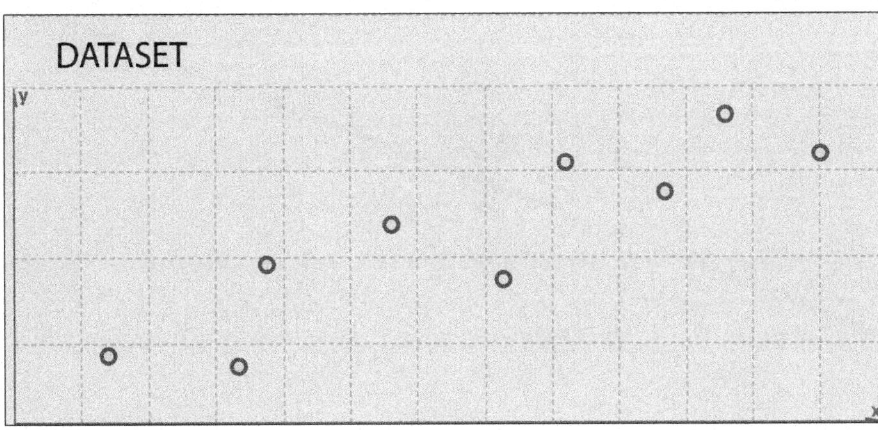

Let's say the goal is to divide this two-dimensional data into one dimension. The way to do that would be to find a line on which we can project this data. Let's find a line that is good for projecting this data on:

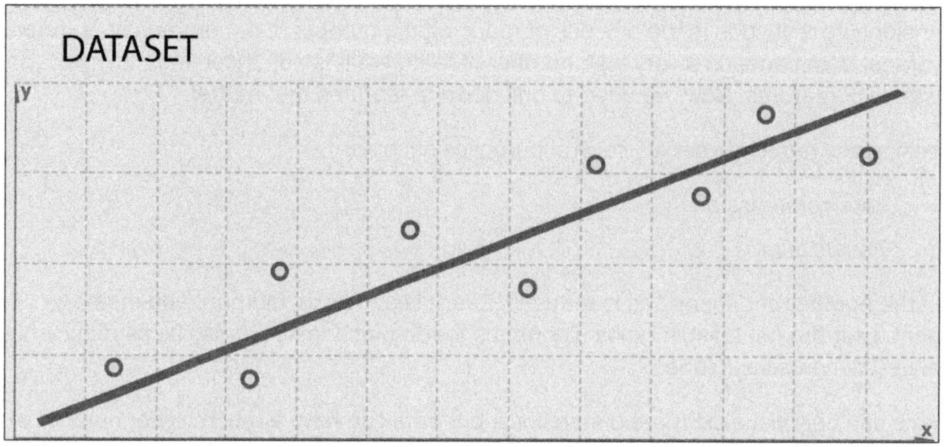

This is the line that has the shortest projected distance from the data points. Let's explain it further by dropping the shortest lines from each data point to this projected line:

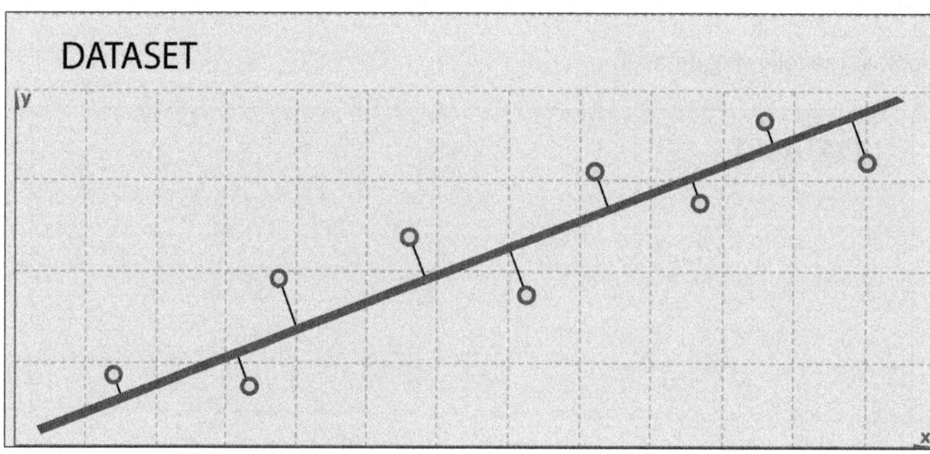

Another way to look at it is that we have to find a line to project the data on so that the sum of the square distances of the data points from this line is minimized. These gray line segments are also called **projection errors**.

Getting ready

Let's look at the three features of the housing data of the City of Saratoga, CA—that is, house size, lot size, and price. Using PCA, we will merge the house size and lot size features into one feature— *z*. Let's call this feature **z density of a house**.

It is worth noting that it is not always possible to give meaning to the new feature created. In this case, it is easy as we have only two features to combine and we can use our common sense to combine the effect of the two. In a more practical case, you may have 1,000 features that you are trying to project to 100 features. It may not be possible to give real-life meaning to each of those 100 features.

In this exercise, we will derive the housing density using PCA and then we will do linear regression to see how this density affects the house price.

There is a preprocessing stage before we delve into PCA: **feature scaling**. Feature scaling comes into the picture when two features have ranges that are at very different scales. Here, house size varies in the range of 800 sq ft to 7,000 sq ft, while the lot size varies between 800 sq ft to a few acres.

Why did we not have to do feature scaling before? The answer is that we really did not have to put features on a level playing field. Gradient descent is another area where feature scaling is very useful.

There are different ways of doing feature scaling:

- Dividing a feature value with a maximum value that will put every feature in the $-1 \le x \le 1$ range
- Dividing a feature value with the range, that is, maximum value - minimum value
- Subtracting a feature value by its mean and then dividing by the range
- Subtracting a feature value by its mean and then dividing by the standard deviation

We are going to use the fourth choice to scale in the best way possible. The following is the data we are going to use for this recipe:

House size	Lot size	Scaled house size	Scaled lot size	House price (in $1,000)
2524	12839	-0.025	-0.231	2405
2937	10000	0.323	-0.4	2200
1778	8040	-0.654	-0.517	1400
1242	13104	-1.105	-0.215	1800

House size	Lot size	Scaled house size	Scaled lot size	House price (in $1,000)
2900	10000	0.291	-0.4	2351
1218	3049	-1.126	-0.814	795
2722	38768	0.142	1.312	2725
2553	16250	-0.001	-0.028	2150
3681	43026	0.949	1.566	2724
3032	44431	0.403	1.649	2675
3437	40000	0.744	1.385	2930
1680	1260	-0.736	-0.92	870
2260	15000	-0.248	-0.103	2210
1660	10032	-0.753	-0.398	1145
3251	12420	0.587	-0.256	2419
3039	69696	0.409	3.153	2750
3401	12600	0.714	-0.245	2035
1620	10240	-0.787	-0.386	1150
876	876	-1.414	-0.943	665
1889	8125	-0.56	-0.512	1430
4406	11792	1.56	-0.294	1920
1885	1512	-0.564	-0.905	1230
1276	1276	-1.077	-0.92	975
3053	67518	0.42	3.023	2400
2323	9810	-0.195	-0.412	1725
3139	6324	0.493	-0.619	2300
2293	12510	-0.22	-0.251	1700
2635	15616	0.068	-0.066	1915
2298	15476	-0.216	-0.074	2278
2656	13390	0.086	-0.198	2497.5
1158	1158	-1.176	-0.927	725
1511	2000	-0.879	-0.876	870
1252	2614	-1.097	-0.84	730
2141	13433	-0.348	-0.196	2050
3565	12500	0.852	-0.251	3330
1368	15750	-0.999	-0.058	1120
5726	13996	2.672	-0.162	4100
2563	10450	0.008	-0.373	1655
1551	7500	-0.845	-0.549	1550

House size	Lot size	Scaled house size	Scaled lot size	House price (in $1,000)
1993	12125	-0.473	-0.274	2100
2555	14500	0.001	-0.132	2100
1572	10000	-0.827	-0.4	1175
2764	10019	0.177	-0.399	2047.5
7168	48787	3.887	1.909	3998
4392	53579	1.548	2.194	2688
3096	10788	0.457	-0.353	2251
2003	11865	-0.464	-0.289	1906

Let's take the scaled house size and scaled house price data and save it as `scaledhousedata.csv`.

How to do it...

1. Load `scaledhousedata.csv` to HDFS:

```
$ hdfs dfs -put scaledhousedata.csv scaledhousedata.csv
```

2. Start the Spark shell:

```
$ spark-shell
```

3. Import statistics and related classes:

```
scala> import org.apache.spark.mllib.linalg.Vectors
scala> import org.apache.spark.mllib.linalg.distributed.RowMatrix
```

4. Load `saratoga.csv` as an RDD:

```
scala> val data = sc.textFile("scaledhousedata.csv")
```

5. Transform the data into an RDD of dense vectors:

```
scala> val parsedData = data.map( line => Vectors.dense(line.
split(',').map(_.toDouble)))
```

6. Create a `RowMatrix` from `parsedData`:

```
scala> val mat = new RowMatrix(parsedData)
```

7. Compute one principal component:

```
scala> val pc= mat.computePrincipalComponents(1)
```

8. Project the rows to the linear space spanned by the principal component:

```
scala> val projected = mat.multiply(pc)
```

9. Convert the projected `RowMatrix` back to the RDD:

```
scala> val projectedRDD = projected.rows
```

10. Save `projectedRDD` back to HDFS:

```
scala> projectedRDD.saveAsTextFile("phdata")
```

Now we will use this projected feature, which we decided to call housing density, plot it against the house price, and see whether any new pattern emerges:

1. Download the HDFS directory `phdata` to the local directory `phdata`:

```
scala> hdfs dfs -get phdata phdata
```

2. Trim start and end brackets in the data and load the data into MS Excel, next to the house price.

The following is the plot of the house price versus the housing density:

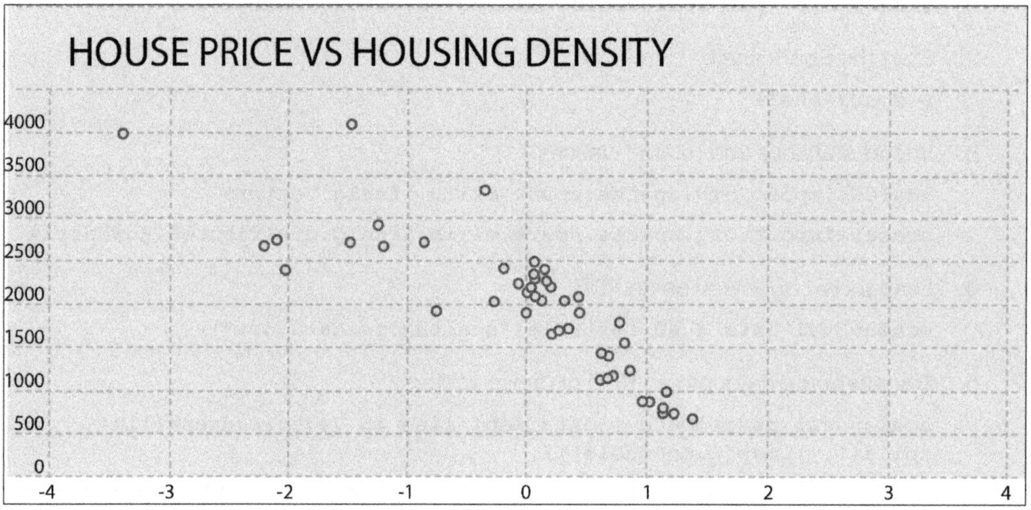

Let's draw some patterns in this data as follows:

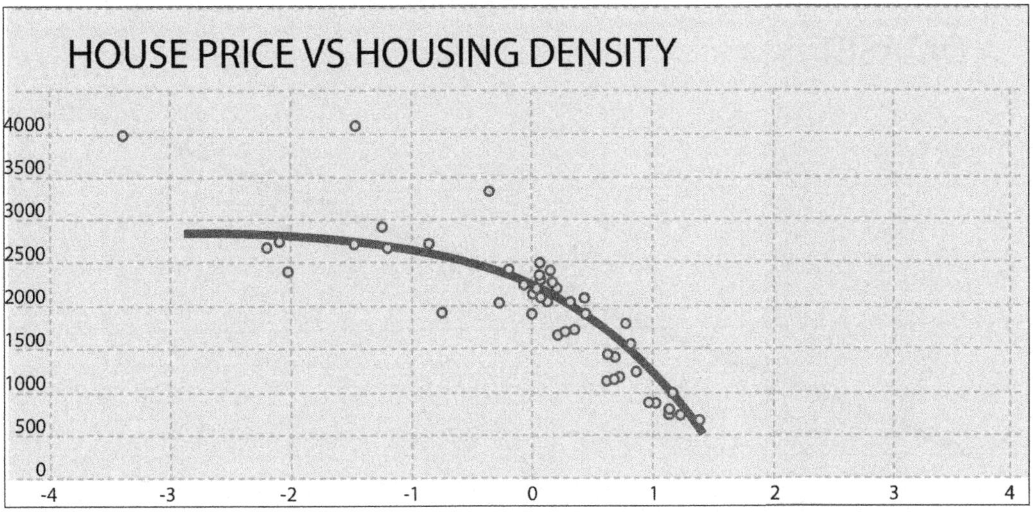

What patterns do we see here? For moving from a very high-density to low-density housing, people are ready to pay a heavy premium. As the housing density reduces, this premium flattens out. For example, people will pay a heavy premium to move from condominiums and town-homes to a single-family home, but the premium on a single- family home with a 3-acre lot size is not going to be much different from a single-family house with a 2-acre lot size in a comparable built-up area.

Dimensionality reduction with singular value decomposition

Often, the original dimensions do not represent data in the best way possible. As we saw in PCA, you can, sometimes, project the data to fewer dimensions and still retain most of the useful information.

Sometimes, the best approach is to align dimensions along the features that exhibit most of the variations. This approach helps to eliminate dimensions that are not representative of the data.

Let's look at the following figure again, which shows the best-fit line on two dimensions:

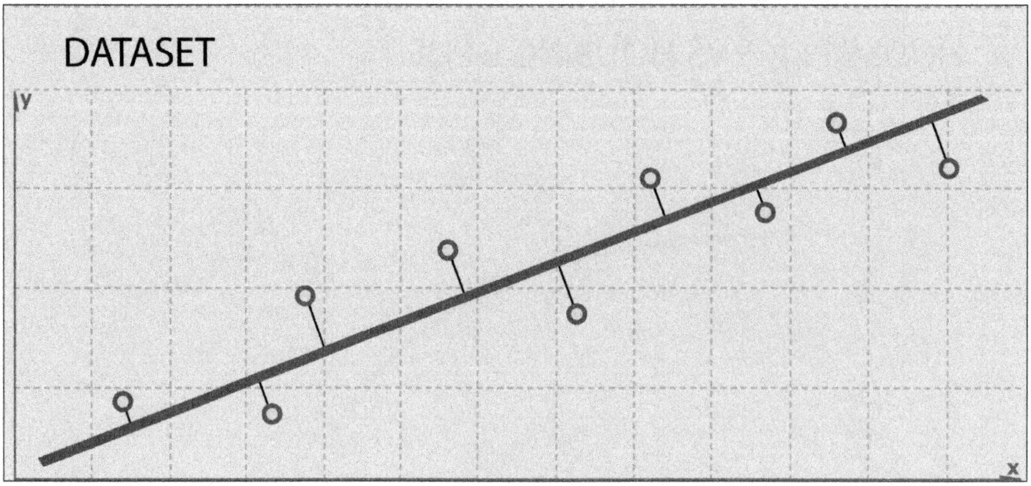

The projection line shows the best approximation of the original data with one dimension. If we take the points where the gray line is intersecting with the black line and isolates the black line, we will have a reduced representation of the original data with as much variation retained as possible, as shown in the following figure:

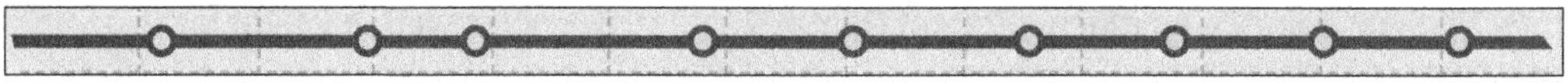

Let's draw a line perpendicular to the first projection line, as shown in the following figure:

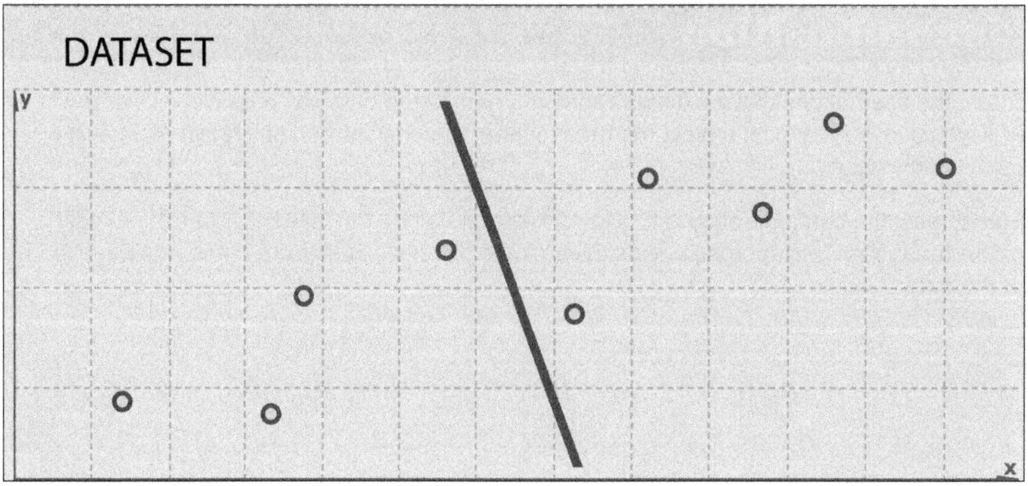

This line captures as much variation as possible along the second dimension of the original dataset. It does a bad job at approximating the original data as this dimension exhibits less variation to start with. It is possible to use these projection lines to generate a set of uncorrelated data points that will show subgroupings in the original data, not visible at first glance.

This is the basic idea behind SVD. Take a high dimension, a highly variable set of data points, and reduce it to a lower dimensional space that exposes the structure of the original data more clearly and orders it from the most variation to the least. What makes SVD very useful, especially for NLP application, is that you can simply ignore variation below a certain threshold to massively reduce the original data, making sure that the original relationship interests are retained.

Let's get slightly into the theory now. SVD is based on a theorem from linear algebra that a rectangular matrix A can be broken down into a product of three matrices—an orthogonal matrix U, a diagonal matrix S, and the transpose of an orthogonal matrix V. We can show it as follows:

$$A = USV^T$$

U and *V* are orthogonal matrices:

$$U^T U = 1$$

$$V^T V = 1$$

The columns of *U* are orthonormal eigenvectors of AA^T and the columns of *V* are orthonormal eigenvectors of $A^T A$. S is a diagonal matrix containing the square roots of eigenvalues from *U* or *V* in descending order.

Getting ready

Let's look at an example of a term-document matrix. We are going to look at two new items about the US presidential elections. The following are the links to the two documents:

- **Fox**: `http://www.foxnews.com/politics/2015/03/08/top-2016-gop-presidential-hopefuls-return-to-iowa-to-hone-message-including/`
- **Npr**: `http://www.npr.org/blogs/itsallpolitics/2015/03/09/391704815/in-iowa-2016-has-begun-at-least-for-the-republican-party`

Let's build the presidential candidate matrix out of these two news items:

$$
\begin{array}{r}
\\
ChrisChristie \\ JebBush \\ MikeHuckabee \\ GeorgePataki \\ RickSantorum \\ LindseyGraham \\ TedCruz \\ ScottWalker \\ RickScott \\ HillaryClinton \\ MarkRubio \\ RickPerry
\end{array}
\begin{array}{c}
npr \quad fox \\
\begin{bmatrix}
1 & 2 \\ 2 & 3 \\ 1 & 4 \\ 1 & 0 \\ 1 & 0 \\ 1 & 3 \\ 1 & 2 \\ 1 & 0 \\ 1 & 2 \\ 0 & 3 \\ 0 & 1 \\ 0 & 2
\end{bmatrix}
\end{array}
$$

Let's put this matrix in a CSV file and then put it in HDFS. We will apply SVD to this matrix and analyze the results.

How to do it...

1. Load `scaledhousedata.csv` to HDFS:

```
$ hdfs dfs -put pres.csv scaledhousedata.csv
```

2. Start the Spark shell:

```
$ spark-shell
```

3. Import statistics and related classes:

```
scala> import org.apache.spark.mllib.linalg.Vectors
scala> import org.apache.spark.mllib.linalg.distributed.RowMatrix
```

4. Load `pres.csv` as an RDD:

```
scala> val data = sc.textFile("pres.csv")
```

5. Transform data into an RDD of dense vectors:

```
scala> val parsedData = data.map( line => Vectors.dense(line.
split(',').map(_.toDouble)))
```

6. Create a `RowMatrix` from `parsedData`:

```
scala> val mat = new RowMatrix(parsedData)
```

7. Compute `svd`:

```
scala> val svd = mat.computeSVD(2,true)
```

8. Calculate the `U` factor (eigenvector):

```
scala> val U = svd.U
```

9. Calculate the matrix of singular values (eigenvalues):

```
scala> val s = svd.s
```

10. Calculate the `V` factor (eigenvector):

```
scala> val s = svd.s
```

If you look at `s`, you will realize that it gave a much higher score to the Npr article than to the Fox article.

10
Recommender Systems

In this chapter, we will cover the following recipes:

- Collaborative filtering using explicit feedback
- Collaborative filtering using implicit feedback

Introduction

The following is Wikipedia's definition of recommender systems:

> *"Recommender systems are a subclass of information filtering system that seek to predict the 'rating' or 'preference' that user would give to an item."*

Recommender systems have gained immense popularity in recent years. Amazon uses them to recommend books, Netflix for movies, and Google News to recommend news stories. As the proof is in the pudding, here are some examples of the impact recommendations can have (source: Celma, Lamere, 2008):

- Two-thirds of the movies watched on Netflix are recommended
- 38 percent of the news clicks on Google News are recommended
- 35 percent of the sales at Amazon sales are the result of recommendations

As we have seen in the previous chapters, features and feature selection play a major role in the efficacy of machine learning algorithms. Recommender engine algorithms discover these features, called **latent features**, automatically. In short, there are latent features responsible for a user to like one movie and dislike another. If another user has corresponding latent features, there is a good chance that this person will also have a similar taste for movies.

To understand this better, let's look at some sample movie ratings:

Movie	Rich	Bob	Peter	Chris
Titanic	5	3	5	?
GoldenEye	3	2	1	5
Toy Story	1	?	2	2
Disclosure	4	4	?	4
Ace Ventura	4	?	4	?

Our goal is to predict the missing entries shown with the ? symbol. Let's see if we can find some features associated with movies. At first, you will look at the genres, as shown here:

Movie	Genre
Titanic	Action, Romance
GoldenEye	Action, Adventure, Thriller
Toy Story	Animation, Children's, Comedy
Disclosure	Drama, Thriller
Ace Ventura	Comedy

Now each movie can be rated for each genre from 0 to 1. For example, *GoldenEye* is not primarily a romance, so it may have 0.1 rating for romance, but 0.98 rating for action. Therefore, each movie can be represented as a feature vector.

> In this chapter, we are going to use the MovieLens dataset from `grouplens.org/datasets/movielens/`.

The InfoObjects big data sandbox comes loaded with 100k movie ratings. From GroupLens you can also download 1 million-or even up to 10 million-ratings if you would like to analyze bigger dataset for better predictions.

We are going to use two files from this dataset:

- `u.data`: This has a tab-separated list of movie ratings in the following format:
  `user id | item id | rating | epoch time`
  Since we are not going to need the time stamp, we are going to filter it out from the data in our recipe

- `u.item`: This has a tab-separated list of movies in the following format:

```
movie id | movie title | release date | video release date |
IMDb URL | unknown | Action | Adventure | Animation |
Children's | Comedy | Crime | Documentary | Drama | Fantasy
|              Film-Noir | Horror | Musical | Mystery | Romance |
Sci-Fi |                Thriller | War | Western |
```

This chapter will cover how we can make recommendations using MLlib, the Spark's machine learning library.

Collaborative filtering using explicit feedback

Collaborative filtering is the most commonly used technique for recommender systems. It has an interesting property—it learns the features on its own. So, in the case of movie ratings, we do not need to provide actual human feedback on whether the movie is romantic or action.

As we saw in the *Introduction* section that movies have some latent features, such as genre, in the same way users have some latent features, such as age, gender, and more. Collaborative filtering does not need them, and figures out latent features on its own.

We are going to use an algorithm called **Alternating Least Squares** (**ALS**) in this example. This algorithm explains the association between a movie and a user based on a small number of latent features. It uses three training parameters: rank, number of iterations, and lambda (explained later in the chapter). The best way to figure out the optimum values of these three parameters is to try different values and see which value has the smallest amount of **Root Mean Square Error** (**RMSE**). This error is like a standard deviation, but it is based on model results rather than actual data.

Getting ready

Upload the `moviedata` downloaded from GroupLens to the `moviedata` folder in `hdfs`:

```
$ hdfs dfs -put moviedata moviedata
```

We are going to add some personalized ratings to this database so that we can test the accuracy of the recommendations.

You can look at `u.item` to pick some movies and rate them. The following are some movies I chose, alongside my ratings. Feel free to choose the movies you would like to rate and provide your own ratings.

Movie ID	Movie name	Rating (1-5)
313	*Titanic*	5
2	*GoldenEye*	3
1	*Toy Story*	1
43	*Disclosure*	4
67	*Ace Ventura*	4
82	*Jurassic Park*	5
96	*Terminator 2*	5
121	*Independence Day*	4
148	*The Ghost and the Darkness*	4

The highest user ID is 943, so we are going to add the new user as 944. Let's create a new comma-separated file `p.data` with the following data:

```
944,313,5
944,2,3
944,1,1
944,43,4
944,67,4
944,82,5
944,96,5
944,121,4
944,148,4
```

How to do it...

1. Upload the personalized movie data to `hdfs`:

   ```
   $ hdfs dfs -put p.data p.data
   ```

2. Import the ALS and rating classes:

   ```
   scala> import org.apache.spark.mllib.recommendation.ALS
   scala> import org.apache.spark.mllib.recommendation.Rating
   ```

3. Load the rating data into an RDD:

   ```
   scala> val data = sc.textFile("moviedata/u.data")
   ```

4. Transform the `val data` into the RDD of rating:

```
scala> val ratings = data.map { line =>
  val Array(userId, itemId, rating, _) = line.split("\t")
  Rating(userId.toInt, itemId.toInt, rating.toDouble)
}
```

5. Load the personalized rating data into the RDD:

```
scala> val pdata = sc.textFile("p.data")
```

6. Transform the data into the RDD of personalized rating:

```
scala> val pratings = pdata.map { line =>
  val Array(userId, itemId, rating) = line.split(",")
  Rating(userId.toInt, itemId.toInt, rating.toDouble)
}
```

7. Combine ratings with personalized ratings:

```
scala> val movieratings = ratings.union(pratings)
```

8. Build the model using ALS with rank 5 and 10 iterations and 0.01 as lambda:

```
scala> val model = ALS.train(movieratings, 10, 10, 0.01)
```

9. Let's predict what my rating would be for a given movie based on this model.
10. Let's start with original *Terminator* with movie ID 195:

```
scala> model.predict(sc.parallelize(Array((944,195)))).collect.
foreach(println)
Rating(944,195,4.198642954004738)
```

Since I rated *Terminator 2* 5, this is a reasonable prediction.

11. Let's try *Ghost* with movie ID 402:

```
scala> model.predict(sc.parallelize(Array((944,402)))).collect.
foreach(println)
Rating(944,402,2.982213836456829)
```

It's a reasonable guess.

12. Let's try *The Ghost and the Darkness*, the movie I already rated, with the ID 148:

```
scala> model.predict(sc.parallelize(Array((944,402)))).collect.
foreach(println)
Rating(944,148,3.8629938805450035)
```

Very close prediction, knowing that I rated the movie 4.

You can use more movies to the `train` dataset. There are also 1 million and 10 million rating datasets available that will refine the algorithm even more.

Collaborative filtering using implicit feedback

Sometimes the feedback available is not in the form of ratings but in the form of audio tracks played, movies watched, and so on. This data, at first glance, may not look as good as explicit ratings by users, but this is much more exhaustive.

Getting ready

We are going to use million song data from `http://www.kaggle.com/c/msdchallenge/data`. You need to download three files:

- `kaggle_visible_evaluation_triplets`
- `kaggle_users.txt`
- `kaggle_songs.txt`

Now perform the following steps:

1. Create a `songdata` folder in `hdfs` and put all the three files here:

   ```
   $ hdfs dfs -mkdir songdata
   ```

2. Upload the song data to `hdfs`:

   ```
   $ hdfs dfs -put kaggle_visible_evaluation_triplets.txt songdata/
   $ hdfs dfs -put kaggle_users.txt songdata/
   $ hdfs dfs -put kaggle_songs.txt songdata/
   ```

We still need to do some more preprocessing. ALS in MLlib takes both user and product IDs as integer. The `Kaggle_songs.txt` file has song IDs and sequence number next to it, The `Kaggle_users.txt` file does not have it. Our goal is to replace the `userid` and `songid` in `triplets` data with the corresponding integer sequence numbers. To do this, follow these steps:

1. Load the `kaggle_songs` data as an RDD:

   ```
   scala> val songs = sc.textFile("songdata/kaggle_songs.txt")
   ```

2. Load the user data as an RDD:

   ```
   scala> val users = sc.textFile("songdata/kaggle_users.txt")
   ```

3. Load the triplets (user, song, plays) data as an RDD:

   ```
   scala> val triplets = sc.textFile("songdata/kaggle_visible_
   evaluation_triplets.txt")
   ```

4. Convert the song data into the `PairRDD`:

```
scala> val songIndex = songs.map(_.split("\\W+")).map(v =>
(v(0),v(1).toInt))
```

5. Collect the `songIndex` as Map:

```
scala> val songMap = songIndex.collectAsMap
```

6. Convert the user data into the `PairRDD`:

```
scala> val userIndex = users.zipWithIndex.map( t => (t._1,t._2.
toInt))
```

7. Collect the `userIndex` as Map:

```
scala> val userMap = userIndex.collectAsMap
```

We will need both `songMap` and `userMap` to replace `userId` and `songId` in triplets. Spark will automatically make both these maps available on the cluster as needed. This works fine but is expensive to send across the cluster every time it is needed.

A better approach is to use a Spark feature called `broadcast` variables. The `broadcast` variables allow the Spark job to keep a read-only copy of a variable cached on each machine, rather than shipping a copy with each task. Spark distributes broadcast variables using efficient broadcast algorithms, so communication cost over the network is negligible.

As you can guess, both `songMap` and `userMap` are good candidates to be wrapped around the `broadcast` variables. Perform the following steps:

1. Broadcast the `userMap`:

```
scala> val broadcastUserMap = sc.broadcast(userMap)
```

2. Broadcast the `songMap`:

```
scala> val broadcastSongMap = sc.broadcast(songMap)
```

3. Convert the `triplet` into an array:

```
scala> val tripArray = triplets.map(_.split("\\W+"))
```

4. Import the rating:

```
scala> import org.apache.spark.mllib.recommendation.Rating
```

5. Convert the `triplet` array into an RDD of rating objects:

```
scala> val ratings = tripArray.map { case Array(user, song, plays)
=>
  val userId = broadcastUserMap.value.getOrElse(user, 0)
  val songId = broadcastUserMap.value.getOrElse(song, 0)
  Rating(userId, songId, plays.toDouble)
}
```

Now, our data is ready to do the modeling and prediction.

How to do it...

1. Import ALS:

```
scala> import org.apache.spark.mllib.recommendation.ALS
```

2. Build a model using the ALS with rank 10 and 10 iterations:

```
scala> val model = ALS.trainImplicit(ratings, 10, 10)
```

3. Extract the user and song tuples from the triplet:

```
scala> val usersSongs = ratings.map( r => (r.user, r.product) )
```

4. Make predictions for the user and song tuples:

```
scala> val predictions = model.predict(usersSongs)
```

How it works...

Our model takes four parameters to work, as shown here:

Parameter name	Description
Rank	Number of latent features in the model
Iterations	Number of iterations for this factorization to run
Lambda	Over fitting parameter
Alpha	Relative weight of observed interactions

As you saw in the case of gradient descent, these parameters need to be set by hand. We can try different values, but the value that works best is rank=50, iterations=30, lambda=0.00001, and alpha= 40.

There's more...

One way to test different parameters quickly is to spawn a spark cluster on Amazon EC2. This gives you flexibility to go with a powerful instance to test these parameters fast. I have created a public s3 bucket `com.infoobjects.songdata` to pull data to Spark.

Here are the steps you need to follow to load the data from S3 and run the ALS:

```
sc.hadoopConfiguration.set("fs.s3n.awsAccessKeyId", "<your access key>")
sc.hadoopConfiguration.set("fs.s3n.awsSecretAccessKey","<your secret key>")
```

```
val songs = sc.textFile("s3n://com.infoobjects.songdata/kaggle_songs.
txt")
val users = sc.textFile("s3n://com.infoobjects.songdata/kaggle_users.
txt")
val triplets = sc.textFile("s3n://com.infoobjects.songdata/kaggle_
visible_evaluation_triplets.txt")
val songIndex = songs.map(_.split("\\W+")).map(v => (v(0),v(1).toInt))
val songMap = songIndex.collectAsMap
val userIndex = users.zipWithIndex.map( t => (t._1,t._2.toInt))
val userMap = userIndex.collectAsMap
val broadcastUserMap = sc.broadcast(userMap)
val broadcastSongMap = sc.broadcast(songMap)
val tripArray = triplets.map(_.split("\\W+"))
import org.apache.spark.mllib.recommendation.Rating
val ratings = tripArray.map{ v =>
  val userId: Int = broadcastUserMap.value.get(v(0)).fold(0)(num => num)
  val songId: Int = broadcastSongMap.value.get(v(1)).fold(0)(num => num)
  Rating(userId,songId,v(2).toDouble)
  }
import org.apache.spark.mllib.recommendation.ALS
val model = ALS.trainImplicit(ratings, 50, 30, 0.000001, 40)
val usersSongs = ratings.map( r => (r.user, r.product) )
val predictions =model.predict(usersSongs)
```

These are the predictions made on the `usersSongs` matrix.

11
Graph Processing Using GraphX

This chapter will cover how we can do graph processing using GraphX, Spark's graph processing library.

The chapter is divided into the following recipes:

- Fundamental operations on graphs
- Using PageRank
- Finding connected components
- Performing neighborhood aggregation

Introduction

Graph analysis is much more commonplace in our life than we think. To take the most common example, when we ask a GPS to find the shortest route to a destination, it uses a graph-processing algorithm.

Let's start by understanding graphs. A graph is a representation of a set of vertices where some pairs of vertices are connected by edges. When these edges move from one direction to another, it's called a **directed graph** or **digraph**.

GraphX is the Spark API for graph processing. It provides a wrapper around an RDD called **resilient distributed property graph**. The property graph is a directed multigraph with properties attached to each vertex and edge.

There are two types of graphs–directed graphs (digraphs) and regular graphs. Directed graphs have edges that run in one direction, for example, from vertex A to vertex B. Twitter follower is a good example of a digraph. If John is David's Twitter follower, it does not mean that David is John's follower. On the other hand, Facebook is a good example of a regular graph. If John is David's Facebook friend, David is also John's Facebook friend.

A multigraph is a graph which is allowed to have multiple edges (also called **parallel edges**). Since every edge in GraphX has properties, each edge has its own identity.

Traditionally, for distributed graph processing, there have been two types of systems:

- Data parallel
- Graph parallel

GraphX aims to combine the two together in one system. GraphX API enables users to view the data both as graphs and as collections (RDDs) without data movement.

Fundamental operations on graphs

In this recipe, we will learn how to create graphs and do basic operations on them.

Getting ready

As a starting example, we will have three vertices, each representing the city center of three cities in California–Santa Clara, Fremont, and San Francisco. The following is the distance between these cities:

Source	Destination	Distance (miles)
Santa Clara, CA	Fremont, CA	20
Fremont, CA	San Francisco, CA	44
San Francisco, CA	Santa Clara, CA	53

How to do it...

1. Import the GraphX-related classes:

```
scala> import org.apache.spark.graphx._
scala> import org.apache.spark.rdd.RDD
```

2. Load the vertex data in an array:

```
scala> val vertices = Array((1L, ("Santa Clara","CA")),(2L,
("Fremont","CA")),(3L, ("San Francisco","CA")))
```

3. Load the array of vertices into the RDD of vertices:

```
scala> val vrdd = sc.parallelize(vertices)
```

4. Load the edge data in an array:

```
scala> val edges = Array(Edge(1L,2L,20),Edge(2L,3L,44),Edge(3L,
1L,53))
```

5. Load the data into the RDD of edges:

```
scala> val erdd = sc.parallelize(edges)
```

6. Create the graph:

```
scala> val graph = Graph(vrdd,erdd)
```

7. Print all the vertices of the graph:

```
scala> graph.vertices.collect.foreach(println)
```

8. Print all the edges of the graph:

```
scala> graph.edges.collect.foreach(println)
```

9. Print the edge triplets; a triplet is created by adding source and destination attributes to an edge:

```
scala> graph.triplets.collect.foreach(println)
```

10. In-degree of a graph is the number of inward-directed edges it has. Print the in-degree of each vertex (as `VertexRDD[Int]`):

```
scala> graph.inDegrees
```

Using PageRank

PageRank measures the importance of each vertex in a graph. PageRank was started by Google's founders, who used the theory that the most important pages on the Internet are the pages with the most links leading to them. PageRank also looks at the importance of a page leading to the target page. So, if a given web page has incoming links from higher rank pages, it will be ranked higher.

Getting ready

We are going to use Wikipedia page link data to calculate page rank. Wikipedia publishes its data in the form of a database dump. We are going to use link data from `http://haselgrove.id.au/wikipedia.htm`, which has the data in two files:

- `links-simple-sorted.txt`
- `titles-sorted.txt`

I have put both of them on Amazon S3 at `s3n://com.infoobjects.wiki/links` and `s3n://com.infoobjects.wiki/nodes`. Since the data size is larger, it is recommended that you run it on either Amazon EC2 or your local cluster. Sandbox may be very slow.

You can load the files to `hdfs` using the following commands:

```
$ hdfs dfs -mkdir wiki
$ hdfs dfs -put links-simple-sorted.txt wiki/links.txt
$ hdfs dfs -put titles-sorted.txt wiki/nodes.txt
```

How to do it...

1. Import the GraphX related classes:

```
scala> import org.apache.spark.graphx._
```

2. Load the edges from `hdfs` with 20 partitions:

```
scala> val edgesFile = sc.textFile("wiki/links.txt",20)
```

Or, load the edges from Amazon S3:

```
scala> val edgesFile = sc.textFile("s3n:// com.infoobjects.wiki/
links",20)
```

> The `links` file has links in the "sourcelink: link1 link2 ..." format.

3. Flatten and convert it into an RDD of "link1,link2" format and then convert it into an RDD of `Edge` objects:

```
scala> val edges = edgesFile.flatMap { line =>
   val links = line.split("\\W+")
   val from = links(0)
     val to = links.tail
   for ( link <- to) yield (from,link)
    }.map( e => Edge(e._1.toLong,e._2.toLong,1))
```

4. Load the vertices from `hdfs` with 20 partitions:

```
scala> val verticesFile = sc.textFile("wiki/nodes.txt",20)
```

5. Or, load the edges from Amazon S3:

```
scala> val verticesFile = sc.textFile("s3n:// com.infoobjects.
wiki/nodes",20)
```

6. Provide an index to the vertices and then swap it to make it in the (index, title) format:

```
scala> val vertices = verticesFile.zipWithIndex.map(_.swap)
```

7. Create the `graph` object:

```
scala> val graph = Graph(vertices,edges)
```

8. Run PageRank and get the vertices:

```
scala> val ranks = graph.pageRank(0.001).vertices
```

9. As ranks is in the (vertex ID, pagerank) format, swap it to make it in the (pagerank, vertex ID) format:

```
scala> val swappedRanks = ranks.map(_.swap)
```

10. Sort to get the highest ranked pages first:

```
scala> val sortedRanks = swappedRanks.sortByKey(false)
```

11. Get the highest ranked page:

```
scala> val highest = sortedRanks.first
```

12. The preceding command gives the vertex id, which you still have to look up to see the actual title with rank. Let's do a join:

```
scala> val join = sortedRanks.join(vertices)
```

13. Sort the joined RDD again after converting from the (vertex ID, (page rank, title)) format to the (page rank, (vertex ID, title)) format:

```
scala> val final = join.map ( v => (v._2._1, (v._1,v._2._2))).
sortByKey(false)
```

14. Print the top five ranked pages

```
scala> final.take(5).collect.foreach(println)
```

Here's what the output should be:

```
(12406.054646736622,(5302153,United_States'_Country_Reports_on_Human_
Rights_Practices))
(7925.094429748747,(84707,2007,_Canada_budget)) (7635.6564216408515,(8
8822,2008,_Madrid_plane_crash)) (7041.479913258444,(1921890,Geographic_
coordinates)) (5675.169862343964,(5300058,United_Kingdom's))
```

Finding connected components

A connected component is a subgraph (a graph whose vertices are a subset of the vertex set of the original graph and whose edges are a subset of the edge set of the original graph) in which any two vertices are connected to each other by an edge or a series of edges.

An easy way to understand it would be by taking a look at the road network graph of Hawaii. This state has numerous islands, which are not connected by roads. Within each island, most roads will be connected to each other. The goal of finding the connected components is to find these clusters.

The connected components algorithm labels each connected component of the graph with the ID of its lowest-numbered vertex.

Getting ready

We will build a small graph here for the clusters we know and use connected components to segregate them. Let's look at the following data:

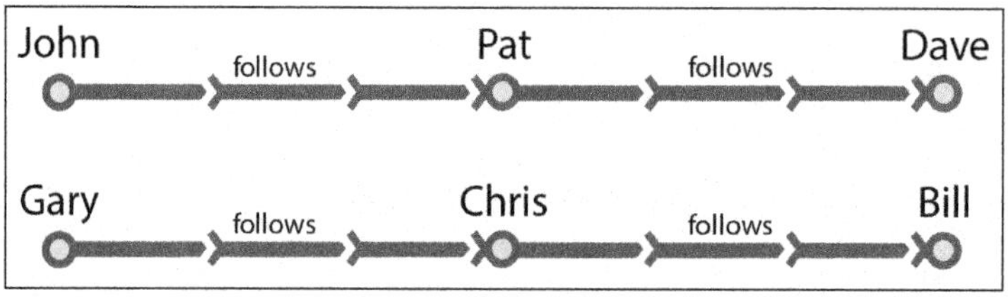

Follower	Followee
John	Pat
Pat	Dave
Gary	Chris
Chris	Bill

The preceding data is a simple one with six vertices and two clusters. Let's put this data in the form of two files: `nodes.csv` and `edges.csv`.

The following is the content of `nodes.csv`:

```
1,John
2,Pat
3,Dave
4,Gary
5,Chris
6,Bill
```

The following is the content of `edges.csv`:

```
1,2,follows
2,3,follows
4,5,follows
5,6,follows
```

We should expect a connected component algorithm to identify two clusters, the first one identified by (1,John) and the second by (4,Gary).

You can load the files to `hdfs` using the following commands:

```
$ hdfs dfs -mkdir data/cc
$ hdfs dfs -put nodes.csv data/cc/nodes.csv
$ hdfs dfs -put edges.csv data/cc/edges.csv
```

How to do it...

1. Load the Spark shell:

   ```
   $ spark-shell
   ```

2. Import the GraphX-related classes:

   ```
   scala> import org.apache.spark.graphx._
   ```

3. Load the edges from `hdfs`:

   ```
   scala> val edgesFile = sc.textFile("hdfs://localhost:9000/user/
   hduser/data/cc/edges.csv")
   ```

4. Convert the `edgesFile` RDD into the RDD of edges:

   ```
   scala> val edges = edgesFile.map(_.split(",")).map(e => Edge(e(0).
   toLong,e(1).toLong,e(2)))
   ```

5. Load the vertices from `hdfs`:

   ```
   scala> val verticesFile = sc.textFile("hdfs://localhost:9000/user/
   hduser/data/cc/nodes.csv")
   ```

6. Map the vertices:

   ```
   scala> val vertices = verticesFile.map(_.split(",")).map( e =>
   (e(0).toLong,e(1)))
   ```

7. Create the `graph` object:

   ```
   scala> val graph = Graph(vertices,edges)
   ```

8. Calculate the connected components:

   ```
   scala> val cc = graph.connectedComponents
   ```

9. Find the vertices for the connected components (which is a subgraph):

   ```
   scala> val ccVertices = cc.vertices
   ```

10. Print the `ccVertices`:

   ```
   scala> ccVertices.collect.foreach(println)
   ```

As you can see in the output, vertices 1,2,3 are pointing to 1, while 4,5,6 are pointing to 4. Both of these are the lowest-indexed vertices in their respective clusters.

Performing neighborhood aggregation

GraphX does most of the computation by isolating each vertex and its neighbors. It makes it easier to process the massive graph data on distributed systems. This makes the neighborhood operations very important. GraphX has a mechanism to do it at each neighborhood level in the form of the `aggregateMessages` method. It does it in two steps:

1. In the first step (first function of the method), messages are send to the destination vertex or source vertex (similar to the Map function in MapReduce).
2. In the second step (second function of the method), aggregation is done on these messages (similar to the Reduce function in MapReduce).

Getting ready

Let's build a small dataset of the followers:

Follower	Followee
John	Barack
Pat	Barack
Gary	Barack
Chris	Mitt
Rob	Mitt

Our goal is to find out how many followers each node has. Let's load this data in the form of two files: `nodes.csv` and `edges.csv`.

The following is the content of `nodes.csv`:

```
1,Barack
2,John
3,Pat
4,Gary
5,Mitt
```

```
6,Chris
7,Rob
```

The following is the content of `edges.csv`:

```
2,1,follows
3,1,follows
4,1,follows
6,5,follows
7,5,follows
```

You can load the files to `hdfs` using the following commands:

```
$ hdfs dfs -mkdir data/na
$ hdfs dfs -put nodes.csv data/na/nodes.csv
$ hdfs dfs -put edges.csv data/na/edges.csv
```

How to do it...

1. Load the Spark shell:

   ```
   $ spark-shell
   ```

2. Import the GraphX related classes:

   ```
   scala> import org.apache.spark.graphx._
   ```

3. Load the edges from `hdfs`:

   ```
   scala> val edgesFile = sc.textFile("hdfs://localhost:9000/user/
   hduser/data/na/edges.csv")
   ```

4. Convert the edges into the RDD of edges:

   ```
   scala> val edges = edgesFile.map(_.split(",")).map(e => Edge(e(0).
   toLong,e(1).toLong,e(2)))
   ```

5. Load the vertices from `hdfs`:

   ```
   scala> val verticesFile = sc.textFile("hdfs://localhost:9000/user/
   hduser/data/cc/nodes.csv")
   ```

6. Map the vertices:

   ```
   scala> val vertices = verticesFile.map(_.split(",")).map( e =>
   (e(0).toLong,e(1)))
   ```

7. Create the `graph` object:

   ```
   scala> val graph = Graph(vertices,edges)
   ```

8. Do the neighborhood aggregation by sending messages to the followees with the number of followers from each follower, that is, 1 and then adding the number of followers:

   ```
   scala> val followerCount = graph.aggregateMessages[(Int)]( t =>
   t.sendToDst(1), (a, b) => (a+b))
   ```

9. Print `followerCount` in the form of (followee, number of followers):

   ```
   scala> followerCount.collect.foreach(println)
   ```

You should get an output similar to the following:

```
(1,3)
(5,2)
```

12
Optimizations and Performance Tuning

This chapter covers various optimizations and performance-tuning best practices when working with Spark.

The chapter is divided into the following recipes:

- Optimizing memory
- Using compression to improve performance
- Using serialization to improve performance
- Optimizing garbage collection
- Optimizing the level of parallelism
- Understanding the future of optimization – project Tungsten

Introduction

Before looking into various ways to optimize Spark, it is a good idea to look at the Spark internals. So far, we have looked at Spark at higher level, where focus was the functionality provided by the various libraries.

Let's start with redefining an RDD. Externally, an RDD is a distributed immutable collection of objects. Internally, it consists of the following five parts:

- Set of partitions (`rdd.getPartitions`)
- List of dependencies on parent RDDs (`rdd.dependencies`)
- Function to compute a partition, given its parents

- Partitioner (optional) (`rdd.partitioner`)
- Preferred location of each partition (optional) (`rdd.preferredLocations`)

The first three are needed for an RDD to be recomputed, in case the data is lost. When combined, it is called **lineage**. The last two parts are optimizations.

A set of partitions is how data is divided into nodes. In case of HDFS, it means `InputSplits`, which are mostly the same as block (except when a record crosses block boundaries; in that case, it will be slightly bigger than a block).

Let's revisit our `wordCount` example to understand these five parts. This is how the RDD graph looks for `wordCount` at dataset level view:

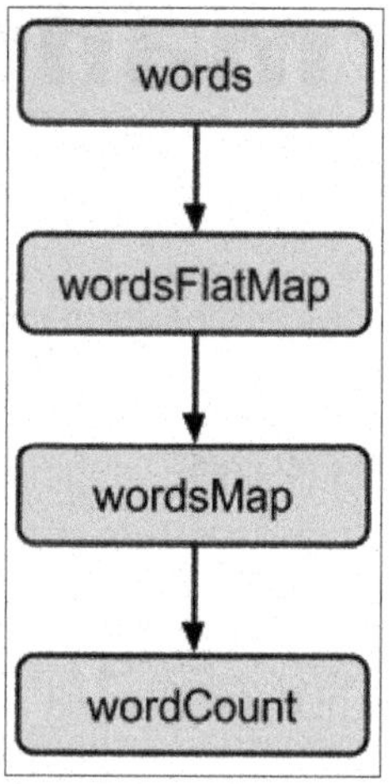

Basically, this is how the flow goes:

1. Load the `words` folder as an RDD:

   ```
   scala> val words = sc.textFile("hdfs://localhost:9000/user/hduser/
   words")
   ```

   The following are the five parts of `words` RDD:

Partitions	One partition per hdfs inputsplit/block (`org.apache.spark.rdd.HadoopPartition`)
Dependencies	None
Compute function	Read the block
Preferred location	The hdfs block location
Partitioner	None

2. Tokenize the words from `words` RDD with each word on a separate line:

```
scala> val wordsFlatMap = words.flatMap(_.split("\\W+"))
```

The following are the five parts of `wordsFlatMap` RDD:

Partitions	Same as parent RDD, that is, `words` (`org.apache.spark.rdd.HadoopPartition`)
Dependencies	Same as parent RDD, that is, `words` (`org.apache.spark.OneToOneDependency`)
Compute function	Compute parent and split each element and flattens the results
Preferred location	Ask parent
Partitioner	None

3. Transform each word in `wordsFlatMap` RDD to (word,1) tuple:

```
scala> val wordsMap = wordsFlatMap.map( w => (w,1))
```

The following are the five parts of `wordsMap` RDD:

Partitions	Same as parent RDD, that is, wordsFlatMap (org.apache.spark.rdd.HadoopPartition)
Dependencies	Same as parent RDD, that is, wordsFlatMap (org.apache.spark.OneToOneDependency)
Compute function	Compute parent and map it to PairRDD
Preferred Location	Ask parent
Partitioner	None

4. Reduce all the values for a given key and sum them up:

```
scala> val wordCount = wordsMap.reduceByKey(_+_)
```

The following are the five parts of `wordCount` RDD:

Partitions	One per reduce task (`org.apache.spark.rdd.ShuffledRDDPartition`)
Dependencies	Shuffle dependency on each parent (`org.apache.spark.ShuffleDependency`)
Compute function	Do addition on shuffled data
Preferred location	None
Partitioner	HashPartitioner (`org.apache.spark.HashPartitioner`)

This is how an RDD graph for `wordCount` looks at the partition level view:

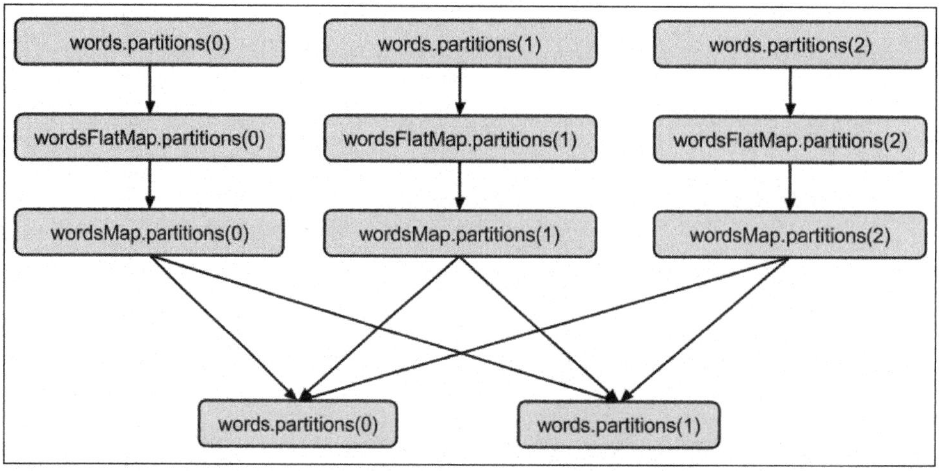

Optimizing memory

Spark is a complex distributed computing framework, and has many moving parts. Various cluster resources, such as memory, CPU, and network bandwidth, can become bottlenecks at various points. As Spark is an in-memory compute framework, the impact of the memory is the biggest.

Another issue is that it is common for Spark applications to use a huge amount of memory, sometimes more than 100 GB. This amount of memory usage is not common in traditional Java applications.

In Spark, there are two places where memory optimization is needed, and that is at the driver and at the executor level.

You can use the following commands to set the driver memory:

- Spark shell:

  ```
  $ spark-shell --drive-memory 4g
  ```

- Spark submit:

  ```
  $ spark-submit --drive-memory 4g
  ```

You can use the following commands to set the executor memory:

- Spark shell:

  ```
  $ spark-shell --executor-memory 4g
  ```

- Spark submit:

  ```
  $ spark-submit --executor-memory 4g
  ```

To understand memory optimization, it is a good idea to understand how memory management works in Java. Objects reside in Heap in Java. Heap is created when JVM starts, and it can resize itself when needed (based on minimum and maximum size, that is, `-Xms` and `-Xmx`, respectively assigned in configuration).

Heap is divided into two spaces or generations: young space and old space. The young space is reserved for the allocation of new objects. Young space consists of an area called **Eden** and two smaller survivor spaces. When the nursery becomes full, garbage is collected by running a special process called **young collection**, where all the objects, which have lived long enough, are promoted to old space. When the old space becomes full, the garbage is collected there by running a process called **old collection**.

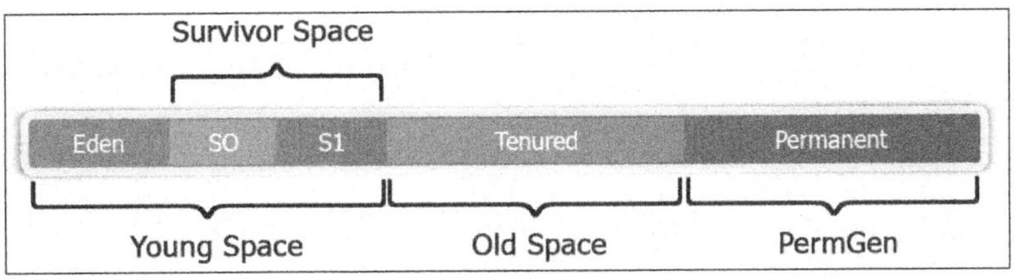

The logic behind nursery is that most objects have a very short life span. A young collection is designed to be fast at finding newly allocated objects and moving them to the old space.

The JVM uses mark and sweep algorithm for garbage collection. Mark and sweep collection consists of two phases.

During the mark phase, all the objects, which have live references, are marked alive, the rest are presumed candidates for garbage collection. During the sweep phase, the space occupied by garbage collectable candidates is added to the free list, that is, they are available to be allocated to new objects.

There are two improvements to mark and sweep. One is **concurrent mark and sweep** (**CMS**) and the other is parallel mark and sweep. CMS focuses on lower latency, while the latter focuses on higher throughput. Both strategies have performance trade-offs. CMS does not do compaction, while parallel **garbage collector** (**GC**) performs whole-heap only compaction, which results in pause times. As a thumb rule, for real-time streaming, CMS should be used, and parallel GC otherwise.

If you would like to have both low latency and high throughput, Java 1.7 update 4 onwards has another option called **garbage-first GC** (**G1**). G1 is a server-style garbage collector, primarily meant for multicore machines with large memories. It is planned as a long-term replacement for CMS. So, to modify our thumb rule, if you are using Java 7 onwards, simply use G1.

G1 partitions the heap into a set of equal-sized regions, where each set is a contiguous range of virtual memory. Each region is assigned a role like Eden, Survivor, and Old. G1 performs a concurrent global marking phase to determine the live references of objects throughout the heap. After the mark phase is over, G1 knows which regions are mostly empty. It collects in these regions first and this frees the larger amount of memory.

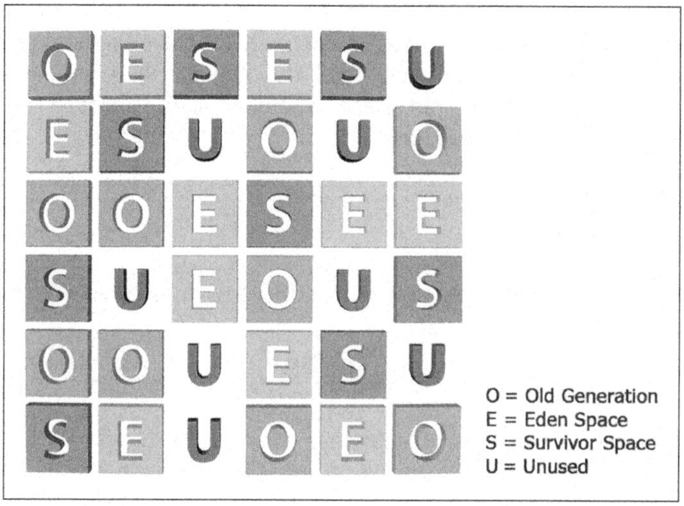

The regions selected by G1 as candidates for garbage collection are garbage collected using evacuation. G1 copies objects from one or more regions of the heap to a single region on the heap, and it both compacts and frees up memory. This evacuation is performed in parallel on multiple cores to reduce pause times and increase throughput. So, each garbage collection round reduces fragmentation while working within user-defined pause times.

There are three aspects in memory optimization in Java:

- Memory footprint
- Cost of accessing objects in memory
- Cost of garbage collection

Java objects, in general, are fast to access but consume much more space than the actual data inside them.

Using compression to improve performance

Data compression involves encoding information using fewer bits than the original representation. Compression has an important role to play in big data technologies. It makes both storage and transport of data more efficient.

When data is compressed, it becomes smaller, so both disk I/O and network I/O become faster. It also saves storage space. Every optimization has a cost, and the cost of compression comes in the form of added CPU cycles to compress and decompress data.

Hadoop needs to split data to put them into blocks, irrespective of whether the data is compressed or not. Only few compression formats are splittable.

Two most popular compression formats for big data loads are LZO and Snappy. Snappy is not splittable, while LZO is. Snappy, on the other hand, is a much faster format.

If compression format is splittable like LZO, input file is first split into blocks and then compressed. Since compression happened at block level, decompression can happen at block level as well as node level.

If compression format is not splittable, compression happens at file level and then it is split into blocks. In this case, blocks have to be merged back to file before they can be decompressed, so decompression cannot happen at node level.

For supported compression formats, Spark will deploy codecs automatically to decompress, and no action is required from the user's side.

Using serialization to improve performance

Serialization plays an important part in distributed computing. There are two persistence (storage) levels, which support serializing RDDs:

- `MEMORY_ONLY_SER`: This stores RDDs as serialized objects. It will create one byte array per partition
- `MEMORY_AND_DISK_SER`: This is similar to the `MEMORY_ONLY_SER`, but it spills partitions that do not fit in the memory to disk

The following are the steps to add appropriate persistence levels:

1. Start the Spark shell:

   ```
   $ spark-shell
   ```

2. Import the `StorageLevel` and implicits associated with it:

   ```
   scala> import org.apache.spark.storage.StorageLevel._
   ```

3. Create an RDD:

```
scala> val words = sc.textFile("words")
```

4. Persist the RDD:

```
scala> words.persist(MEMORY_ONLY_SER)
```

Though serialization reduces the memory footprint substantially, it adds extra CPU cycles due to deserialization.

By default, Spark uses Java's serialization. Since the Java serialization is slow, the better approach is to use `Kryo` library. `Kryo` is much faster and sometimes even 10 times more compact than the default.

How to do it...

You can use `Kryo` by doing the following settings in your `SparkConf`:

1. Start the Spark shell by setting `Kryo` as serializer:

```
$ spark-shell --conf spark.serializer=org.apache.spark.serializer.
KryoSerializer
```

2. `Kryo` automatically registers most of the core Scala classes, but if you would like to register your own classes, you can use the following command:

```
scala> sc.getConf.registerKryoClasses(Array(classOf[com.
infoobjects.CustomClass1],classOf[com.infoobjects.CustomClass2])
```

Optimizing garbage collection

JVM garbage collection can be a challenge if you have a lot of short lived RDDs. JVM needs to go over all the objects to find the ones it needs to garbage collect. The cost of the garbage collection is proportional to the number of objects the GC needs to go through. Therefore, using fewer objects and the data structures that use fewer objects (simpler data structures, such as arrays) helps.

Serialization also shines here as a byte array needs only one object to be garbage collected.

By default, Spark uses 60 percent of the executor memory to cache RDDs and the rest 40 percent for regular objects. Sometimes, you may not need 60 percent for RDDs and can reduce this limit so that more space is available for object creation (less need for GC).

How to do it...

You can set the memory allocated for RDD cache to 40 percent by starting the Spark shell and setting the memory fraction:

```
$ spark-shell --conf spark.storage.memoryFraction=0.4
```

Optimizing the level of parallelism

Optimizing the level of parallelism is very important to fully utilize the cluster capacity. In the case of HDFS, it means that the number of partitions is the same as the number of `InputSplits`, which is mostly the same as the number of blocks.

In this recipe, we will cover different ways to optimize the number of partitions.

How to do it...

Specify the number of partitions when loading a file into RDD with the following steps:

1. Start the Spark shell:

   ```
   $ spark-shell
   ```

2. Load the RDD with a custom number of partitions as a second parameter:

   ```
   scala> sc.textFile("hdfs://localhost:9000/user/hduser/words",10)
   ```

Another approach is to change the default parallelism by performing the following steps:

3. Start the Spark shell with the new value of default parallelism:

   ```
   $ spark-shell --conf spark.default.parallelism=10
   ```

4. Check the default value of parallelism:

   ```
   scala> sc.defaultParallelism
   ```

> You can also reduce the number of partitions using an RDD method called `coalesce(numPartitions)` where `numPartitions` is the final number of partitions you would like. If you would like the data to be reshuffled over the network, you can call the RDD method called `repartition(numPartitions)` where `numPartitions` is the final number of partitions you would like.

Understanding the future of optimization – project Tungsten

Project Tungsten, starting with Spark Version 1.4, is the initiative to bring Spark closer to bare metal. The goal of this project is to substantially improve the memory and CPU efficiency of the Spark applications and push the limits of underlying hardware.

In distributed systems, conventional wisdom has been to always optimize network I/O as that has been the most scarce and bottlenecked resource. This trend has changed in the last few years. Network bandwidth, in the last 5 years, has changed from 1 gigabit per second to 10 gigabit per second.

On similar lines, the disk bandwidth has increased from 50 MB/s to 500 MB/s and SSDs are being deployed more and more. CPU clock speed, on the other hand, was ~3 GHz 5 years back and is still the same. This has unseated the network and made CPU the new bottleneck in distributed processing.

> Another trend that has put more load on CPU performance is the new compressed data formats such as Parquet. Both compression and serialization, as we have seen in the previous recipes in this chapter, lead to more CPU cycles. This trend has also pushed the need for CPU optimization to reduce the CPU cycle cost.

On the similar lines, let's look at the memory footprint. In Java, GC does memory management. GC has done an amazing job at taking away the memory management from the programmer and making it transparent. To do this, Java has to put a lot of overhead, and that substantially increases the memory footprint. As an example, a simple String "abcd", which should ideally take 4 bytes, takes 48 bytes in Java.

What if we do away with GC and manage memory manually like in lower-level programming languages such as C? Java does provide a way to do that since 1.7 version and it is called `sun.misc.Unsafe`. Unsafe essentially means that you can build long regions of memory without any safety checks. This is the first feature of project Tungsten.

Manual memory management by leverage application semantics

Manual memory management by leverage application semantics, which can be very risky if you do not know what you are doing, is a blessing with Spark. We used knowledge of data schema (DataFrames) to directly layout the memory ourselves. It not only gets rid of GC overheads, but lets you minimize the memory footprint.

The second point is storing data in CPU cache versus memory. Everyone knows CPU cache is great as it takes three cycles to get data from the main memory versus one cycle in cache. This is the second feature of project Tungsten.

Using algorithms and data structures

Algorithms and data structures are used to exploit memory hierarchy and enable more cache-aware computation.

CPU caches are small pools of memory that store the data the CPU is going to need next. CPUs have two types of caches: instruction cache and data cache. Data caches are arranged in hierarchy of L1, L2, and L3:

- L1 cache is the fastest and most expensive cache in a computer. It stores the most critical data and is the first place the CPU looks for information.
- L2 cache is slightly slower than L1, but still located on the same processor chip. It is the second place the CPU looks for information.
- L3 cache is still slower, but is shared by all cores, such as DRAM (memory).

These can be seen in the following diagram:

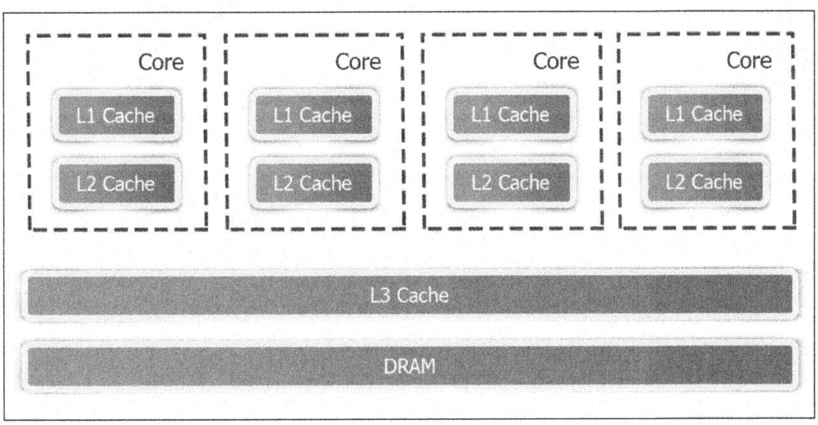

The third point is that Java is not very good at bytecode generation for things like expression evaluation. If this code generation is done manually, it is much more efficient. Code generation is the third feature of project Tungsten.

Code generation

This involves exploiting modern compliers and CPUs to allow efficient operations directly on binary data. Project Tungsten is in its infancy at present and will have much wider support in version 1.5.

Index

D

E

F

G

H

I

J

K

L

M

N

O

P

Q

R

[PACKT] open source
community experience distilled
PUBLISHING

Thank you for buying
Spark Cookbook

About Packt Publishing

Packt, pronounced 'packed', published its first book, *Mastering phpMyAdmin for Effective MySQL Management*, in April 2004, and subsequently continued to specialize in publishing highly focused books on specific technologies and solutions.

Our books and publications share the experiences of your fellow IT professionals in adapting and customizing today's systems, applications, and frameworks. Our solution-based books give you the knowledge and power to customize the software and technologies you're using to get the job done. Packt books are more specific and less general than the IT books you have seen in the past. Our unique business model allows us to bring you more focused information, giving you more of what you need to know, and less of what you don't.

Packt is a modern yet unique publishing company that focuses on producing quality, cutting-edge books for communities of developers, administrators, and newbies alike. For more information, please visit our website at `www.packtpub.com`.

About Packt Open Source

In 2010, Packt launched two new brands, Packt Open Source and Packt Enterprise, in order to continue its focus on specialization. This book is part of the Packt open source brand, home to books published on software built around open source licenses, and offering information to anybody from advanced developers to budding web designers. The Open Source brand also runs Packt's open source Royalty Scheme, by which Packt gives a royalty to each open source project about whose software a book is sold.

Writing for Packt

We welcome all inquiries from people who are interested in authoring. Book proposals should be sent to `author@packtpub.com`. If your book idea is still at an early stage and you would like to discuss it first before writing a formal book proposal, then please contact us; one of our commissioning editors will get in touch with you.

We're not just looking for published authors; if you have strong technical skills but no writing experience, our experienced editors can help you develop a writing career, or simply get some additional reward for your expertise.

Community Experience Distilled
Learning Hadoop 2
Design and implement data processing, lifecycle management, and analytic workflows with the cutting-edge toolbox of Hadoop 2
Garry Turkington
Gabriele Modena
[PACKT] open source

Community Experience Distilled
Big Data Analytics with R and Hadoop
Set up an integrated infrastructure of R and Hadoop to turn your data analytics into Big Data analytics
Vignesh Prajapati
[PACKT] open source

CPSIA information can be obtained
at www.ICGtesting.com
Printed in the USA
FSOW04n1549030815
9469FS

9 781783 987061